All Scripture references taken from the KJV of the Holy Bible, unless otherwise indicated.

LABAN: Defeat Delay, Theft & Trickery

by Dr. Marlene Miles

Freshwater Press 2025

Freshwaterpress9@gmail.com

ISBN: 978-1-971933-07-8

Paperback Version

Copyright 2025, Dr. Marlene Miles

All rights reserved. No part of this book may be reproduced, distributed, or transmitted by any means or in any means including photocopying, recording or other electronic or mechanical methods without prior written permission of the publisher except in the case of brief publications or critical reviews.

Table of Contents

- REBEKAH'S BROTHER 5
- REBEKAH SENDS JACOB TO LABAN 8
- A SISTER'S BROTHER 13
- BETHUEL'S HOUSEHOLD 21
- MANIPULATOR'S MASTERMIND 23
- LIVING WITH MASTER MANIPULATORS 27
- JACOB'S SPIRITUAL LEGACY 33
- LABAN STYLE 35
- WHAT ABOUT YOU? 38
- LABAN VS. JACOB COMPARATIVE CHART 42
- SPOTTING LABAN-TYPES 47
- LABAN vs PHARAOH vs SAUL 54
- WHEN YOUR BLESSING IS IN THE HOUSE OF LABAN 58
- PRAYER FOR DISCERNING THE SEASON OF RELEASE 64
- GOD-LED BREAKAWAYS 66
- 12 SIGNS GOD IS RELEASING YOU 73
- DO NOT RECONNECT 78
- PROPHETIC DECLARATIONS 79
- PROPHETIC ACTIVATION 83

WARFARE PSALM -Against Narcissistic Manipulation & Controlling Spirits 88

DELIVERANCE PRAYER: BREAKING NARCISSISTIC CONTROL 92

WARFARE PSALM For Breaking Soul-Ties............. 97

HOW JACOB BROKE FROM LABAN 101

DELIVERANCE PRAYER FROM LABAN *SPIRITS* .. 103

WARFARE PRAYERS 105

Dear Reader 128

Prayerbooks by this author 129

Other books by this author 131

The Spirit of

LABAN

Defeat: Delay, Theft & Trickery

REBEKAH'S BROTHER

And Rebekah had a brother, and his name was Laban: and Laban ran out unto the man, unto the well.

And it came to pass, when he saw the earring and bracelets upon his sister's hands, and when he heard the words of Rebekah his sister, saying, Thus spake the man unto me; that he came unto the man; and, behold, he stood by the camels at the well.

And he said, Come in, thou blessed of the Lord; wherefore standest thou without? for I have prepared the house, and room for the camels.
(Genesis 24:29-31)

I don't know about you, but I've seen so many shows and heard too many stories of a man being sized up by how much wealth he has, shows or gives. Rebekah's brother said what? First, he took a look at the jewelry and then he said, Come in, thou blessed of the Lord. Abraham's servant who was sent to get a bride for Isaac was immediately invited in, to stay and he and his transportation were cared for.

Rebekah's brother. Laban.

Then Abraham's servant kept talking --

> And he said, I am Abraham's servant. ...And the Lord hath blessed my master greatly; and he is become great: and he hath given him flocks, and herds, and silver, and gold, and menservants, and maidservants, and camels, and asses. (Genesis 24:34-35)

Of course, it was in the plan of God that Isaac would marry Rebekah, but as we learn more about Laban, we can suppose that dollar signs may have registered in his eyes.

Abraham's servant was following the directives given to Abraham from God and they worshipped God. After the servant gave Rebekah the erring (on her face) and the bracelets on her hand, he falls down and worshipped God. Nowhere do we see that Laban or his own father, Bethuel worshipped God; they have had lip speak in this accounting, but they did not fall down and worship God. They just went along with everything as they had been previously told:

> Then Laban and Bethuel answered and said, The thing proceedeth from the Lord: we cannot speak unto thee bad or good. (Genesis 24:50)

And surely the precious gifts—the bride price surely swayed the people, especially the men of this house.

> And the servant brought forth jewels of silver, and jewels of gold, and raiment, and gave them to

Rebekah: he gave also to her brother and to her mother precious things.

And they sent away Rebekah their sister, and her nurse, and Abraham's servant, and his men.

And they blessed Rebekah, and said unto her, Thou art our sister, be thou the mother of thousands of millions, and let thy seed possess the gate of those which hate them. (Genesis 24:53, 60)

They received a hefty bride price for Rebekah, and blessed her and sent her away happy. They spoke what seemed like Godly blessings over her and sent her away to be married to Isaac, the son of Abraham.

REBEKAH SENDS JACOB TO LABAN

Time goes by. Isaac is very pleased with Rebekah and she in the course of time gave birth to twins, Esau and Jacob. After the two boys were grown, and at the time of the passing of Isaac, Jacob, whose name means *supplanter*, tricked Esau out of his birthright. Esau was furious and threatened to kill Jacob. So Rebekah helped Jacob to get away from Esau by sending him to her brother, Laban's house.

> Then Jacob went on his journey, and came into the land of the people of the east.
>
> And he looked, and behold a well in the field, and, lo, there were three flocks of sheep lying by it; for out of that well they watered the flocks: and a great stone was upon the well's mouth.
>
> And he said unto them, Know ye Laban the son of Nahor? And they said, We know him.
>
> And he said unto them, Is he well? And they said, He is well: and, behold, Rachel his daughter cometh with the sheep. (Genesis 29: 1-2, 5-6)

THE MANY CRIMES OF LABAN

Laban looks normal, maybe even kind. He's your relative or a trusted person --, maybe your parent is vouching for him. We are all taught to respect and obey our elders. As kids, we do it—until we learn who they really are; until we learn better. Sometimes if you go into a church, the entire congregation, or most of it is vouching for the leader or the leaders, else why are they still sitting there week after week? Therefore, you believe he, *or they* – the leaders have been vetted.

Jacob came to Laban through Jacob's mother. He's my relative, my uncle, he must be okay. However, Jacob was in a place of desperation because of what he had done to his own relative, his own twin brother, Esau. Because of Esau's drama and hunger, Jacob exploited Esau. When Esau became furious about having been tricked, Jacob fled to their Uncle Laban's ranch.

Laban? He welcomed Jacob and then proceeded to exploit Jacob for 20 years.

Laban is a lot of things and one of those things is that he is an opportunist. But, was not Jacob also that, if not in reality, in proxy, since Jacob's mother Rebekah was an opportunist who put Jacob up to stealing his own brother's birthright.

This is the part everyone remembers — Jacob working 7 years for Rachel, getting Leah instead, then another 7 for Rachel, then 6 more to earn his flock. Laban never meant to let him go. Jacob describes it best:

You changed my wages ten times. (Genesis 31:41)

That's manipulation, exploitation, and financial control all in one. As we look at this story our sentiment quickly shifts to Jacob being the victim. Ironic, Jacob had just victimized someone, yet he wants to be pitied now. Jacob wants to be protected. Jacob wants to be treated well—treated fairly when that is not what he just dished out to Esau when he gave him bean soup. Jacob who has run to Laban's ranch carrying the birthright of the firstborn, trying to hide it--, and Laban, ever the opportunist looks at his own nephew and maybe he sees or says something within himself – this is a very rich man. And, I like rich men because I can exploit them and take from them. And, that's what I will do---, I will take from this man, this Jacob. He's the son of my sister Rebekah and I know how rich her husband and her people are, so sure he can stay here. And, since he's desperate, I must parlay that into something for myself.

Laban used *his own daughters* as bargaining chip--, well that's a nice way of saying it, I'd say he used at least one of his girls as a honey pot. He knew Jacob liked Rachel and he dangled her in front of Jacob who hoped for 14 years to marry Rachel and lay with her. And Jacob was about 140 years old when he married Rachel. So, from age 120 (or so) to age 140, Jacob worked for Rachel.

This is the dark part. Laban didn't treat Rachel or Leah as treasured daughters; he treated them as leverage. He married off Leah deceptively. Then he used Rachel as the "bait" to keep Jacob under his roof.

Laban did control the sexual rights of his daughters—that is a father's responsibility, but he used those rights to his own advantage, not to the advantage of his daughters. He controlled their marriages. He made decisions *about* them without them. T*hey* felt emotionally used and financially robbed by him.

Later, Rachel and Leah themselves say:

Our father has treated us like foreigners… he spent everything he received for us.
(Genesis 31:14–15)

Laban was the cause of the long-lasting marital tension in both of his daughters' marriages – since they were polygamous and married to the same man, Jacob.

One sister can barely borrow another sister's sweater or hoodie, how much more drama will there be when they are dating or trying to date the same man? It's even worse when they are married to the same man. Leah, bragging that by performance she was the real wife, or the better wife. While Rachel knew and bragged that she is the one that Jacob loves, all the while not being able to perform as a wife who produces heirs, for many years.

The rivalry between Rachel and Leah? It didn't start with them. It was seeded by Laban's deception. A man who controls and manipulates will produce that same atmosphere inside his own household. Their jealousy, insecurity, and competition were rooted in how they were introduced into the marriage — as unequal, unwilling rivals.

Laban indirectly set off a chain of emotional and spiritual battles.

Spiritual battles?

Yes. The spirit of Laban is still working today in many ways, messing up people's lives – that makes it spiritual. And it's spiritual because when Jacob and his whole crew finally left Laban's ranch, Rachel took Laban's idols.

A SISTER'S BROTHER

Rebekah & Laban were more alike than we may have realized. one used manipulation for protection. The other used manipulation for profit. But the root was the same; and they both used manipulation, which is witchcraft. Both came from the house of Bethuel of Padan-Aram — a family known for sharp negotiation, quick thinking and hidden agendas. This family was known for managing outcomes to their advantage and protecting their own interests. They displayed the gift of hospitality but used it for opportunism.

Both Rebekah and Laban were very persuasive. Rebekah convinced Jacob to deceive his own father, Isaac, to steal the birthright from his twin brother, Esau. Rebekah was instrumental in managing Esau's reaction. She single-handedly shaped Jacob's destiny through influence, directing every detail, step by step. We are not saying that God was not in this, but in the natural, what Rebekah meant for selfishness and for wrong, God was using it. When God is allowing something, even something that is not particularly Godly, then He is using it.

Rebekah persuades quietly and emotionally.

Laban, her brother, is very convincing as well. They both convinced the same person—Jacob. So, Jacob, since you're here, you can serve 7 years and there is a reward at the end--, Rachel. So, Jacob served for 7 years and didn't get Rachel—he got a substitute-- Leah. But he was convinced to serve 7 more years for the same prize that he was offered the first time—Rachel. Laban convinced Jacob to stay 6 more years and this time for wages (livestock).

This is the perfect set up to an online revenge story: 'Family helps family' – *what?*

Let us remember that Laban was a man of idols—therefore, he used whatever "gifts" the idols provided to him in exchange for his idolatry, his idol worship. Laban persuades through charm, guilt, and deceptive contracts that only benefit Laban—these could very well be the gifts the idols gave for Laban's worship.

Different sibs, different genders, different positions in the family of birth and in Jabob's life, but the same skill. Different motives. Same family. Different siblings.

Both used strategies to control outcomes. Rebekah strategized Jacob into the blessing. She calculated Esau's temperament. She Estimated Isaac's blindness. She outmaneuvered the entire household in a single day. This woman was an evil Chloe from the TV Show 24; she timed Jacob's escape and even had a safe place for him to go. Does it amaze anyone else that she helped her son rip off her other son? How witchy is that?

Laban would not be outdone by his sister – oh no! Laban strategized Leah into the wedding. Sometimes I wonder what did Leah know, and when did she know it? Laban changed Jacob's wages repeatedly. He used superstition (remember he was an idolater) and agreements with fine print and fine-fine print – okay—no print-- to trap him. If it is not in writing, did anyone say that? What did anyone actually agree to. Let me say, when you are talking to a diviner, an idolater, an occultist, a witch—what you are agreeing to may not be what they are talking about at all. What they may have a person agreeing to may not be the subject of the conversation in the natural at all. Yet the victim may be trapped by their own words.

This is akin to saying certain words in a phishing phone call and all of a sudden, you've agreed with something that wasn't asked, or something you know nothing about. It is binding, until you figure it out and get out of the agreement. Pray the Lord that it is in time before much damage or devastation is done.

Laban and Rebekah both timed their confrontations cleverly. The brother and sister operate with the same strategic mind.

Both lied with *deception* when necessary—or just when they felt like it. This is the uncomfortable truth. Rebekah plots Isaac's deception. She changes Jacob's outfit – when you are dealing in the spiritual realm, for good or bad, there will often be a wardrobe change. Rebekah expedites the exchange of destiny for her two sons, and it started with dressing Jacob in goat skins. So, doesn't it make sense that Jacob's sons, later on, would despise Joseph's dream, Joseph's destiny and try to exchange or destroy it? As well, the selling of Joseph involve the removal of a garment?

Rebekah easily rehearses Jacob's lies to his own father. She manipulates timing. She ensures Esau stays unaware.

Laban switches Leah for Rachel. They weren't twins, but Rachel should have been the first wife of Jacob which is a position of honor in polygamous households. Maybe Jacob only wanted one wife, Rachel. He was close to 140 when he married her. If a man is not married by 140, is he looking for a wife? Like, at all? Is he suddenly looking for multiple wives at age 120? What the world calls *karma* and what we call **sow and reap** – Jacob had that switcheroo coming, *didn't he?*

Jacob was dealing with an uncle who hides his true intentions until it's too late. Laban changed labor agreements. He also was an idolater who concealed his idols. Laban pursues Jacob under false pretenses. Their household used deception as either a survival and success tactic—whatever fits the occasion. Rebekah and Laban were both 'quick on their feet' and could read a situation and work it to full advantage.

Both used people they loved, or said they loved – people they were supposed to love to achieve their goals. But isn't that easiest? Those who think you love them, or those who love you will trust you and let down their guards completely.

Rebekah loved Jacob sincerely, but still used him in her plan. Even God said, Jacob have I loved… I guess Esau was hateable and Jacob was loveable.

> As it is written, Jacob have I loved, but Esau have I hated. (Romans 9:13)

Rebekah used Jacob as an instrument – even a weapon. She used him as a solution and her strategic pawn.

Meanwhile, back at the ranch, Laban loved, or was supposed to love his daughters. Laban used them as bargaining chips. He used Rachel (forgive me) as a honey pot). He used them for control and to his advantage. Bait.

Both siblings of Bethuel were quick thinkers under pressure. When Rebekah overhears Isaac, she instantly sees the threat, formulates a plan, directs (manipulates) all actors. She looks ahead to see the consequences and still executes with precision.

On his ranch, when Jacob prospers, Laban instantly shifts the deal back to his own advantage. Laban confronts Jacob, reorganizes the flocks, manipulates his sons, and controls the narrative

Both these siblings were *tacticians. For good or for bad, they are both dangerous.*

Both were deeply family-loyal — to a fault; well at least they appear to be. My theory is that loving people don't manipulate others, especially family members. Especially spouses, especially children and blood relatives. But we do see a form of family loyalty, the two elder sibs didn't do anything directly to one another, but Laban's children and his sister's children were in play.

Rebekah's actions were to protect Jacob. Her loyalty blinded her to the long-term fallout.

Laban's actions were to preserve wealth and control. His loyalty blinded him to the damage he caused Rachel and Leah. Both these siblings are a case study in "the blessings of the Lord maketh rich and He adds no sorrow with it." When the sorrow comes from an action that seemed to have bought favor, wealth, or some other natural outcome, then we will know that God didn't send that.

Family loyalty was their justification for manipulation--, but still, it was manipulation. Each of these siblings had troubling relationships with truth. Neither lied for pleasure; they lied for what they perceived was *purpose*. They had a reason for everything they did— *'what had happened was'* kind of situations. Both saw truth as flexible, negotiable, useful, but not sacred – perhaps as alternative facts. They prioritized outcomes over honesty.

This is a *family trait; Bethuel's house.*

Both impacted Jacob's destiny — for better and for worse. Rebekah shaped Jacob's blessing. She pushed him into prophecy, even if it cost her family peace. Laban shaped Jacob's endurance; He pushed Jacob into maturity, even if it cost him 20 years.

Between the two, Rebekah taught Jacob strategy. Laban taught Jacob strength. God used Laban to teach Jacob how to stand and even how to fight. This is the first time we see Jacob employing witty inventions to get the cattle to multiply according to their colors. He did this himself; it's not like he called his mother to ask her what to do.

However, together, his mother and his uncle forged the character of Israel. Jacob's entire life unfolded between people who loved him and manipulated him at the same time. He was surrounded on both sides, by individuals who were to the positive, sharp thinkers and emotionally intelligent. They each were persuasive and strategic. On the dark side, they were self-serving and deeply loyal to their own interests.

It wasn't coincidence.

Jacob was the product of a household culture—the house of Bethuel in Padan-Aram—where manipulation, negotiation, and cunning were not inherently sins… but *skills until they misused them, then they became sin.* To understand Jacob, you must understand the environment that shaped him.

BETHUEL'S HOUSEHOLD

Rebekah's father, Laban's father — Jacob's maternal grandfather was Bethuel. This patriarch's home sat at the intersection of hospitality, shrewdness, tradition, superstition, family loyalty, opportunistic thinking, get rich, get over, get that bag.

The culture produced brilliant, persuasive people with a few consistent traits. They used hospitality mixed with ulterior motives. This house welcomed travelers — but watched for opportunities. Someone once said to me that they loved meeting new people because that means that another whole new realm would open up. I was suspect.

FYI: Witches can be some of the nicest people in the world. Become weary though when they start questioning you, especially asking you very personal things.

When Abraham's servant arrived for Rebekah, Laban (and likely Bethuel) immediately, sized up those gifts, considered what he might gain from his sister's marriage and then performed kindness with strategy.

Kindness was real. But never without calculation. Remember, they are quick, decisive, strategic thinkers. Rebekah instantly recognized the servant's importance. Laban instantly saw the gold. Bethuel instantly granted permission for the marriage. No hesitation. This family made decisions *fast*.

In a structure where outcomes matter more than process, truth, customs, promises, all were negotiable if it protected the family. They would bend anything necessary to secure advantage, protect their own, preserve wealth, avoid loss, influence outcomes. This shaped Rebekah and Laban. This shaped the entire atmosphere that Jacob, yet unborn, would enter.

Emotional intelligence sharpened into manipulation in that family. They weren't villains—necessarily—well, they didn't kill people. They might argue that they are just survivors, doing what it takes to live day by day. Their emotional intelligence became tactical insight, controlling conversation, persuasive speech, pressure or guilt when needed. They created in people quiet, even subtle obligation, strategic silence.

Bethuel's household was a master class in influence. Family loyalty was elevated above everything. Truth? negotiable. Promises? bendable. But family? Untouchable.

Thus, manipulation wasn't seen as harmful — it was seen as protective. This is the root of everything Jacob experiences when he gets his immersive experience in the House of Bethuel under the eye of his Uncle Laban. For 20 years.

MANIPULATOR'S MASTERMIND

Esau was chaotic, impulsive, emotional, and reactionary. But he was his mother's son as well--, he was also a manipulator. Esau's manipulation wasn't subtle. It was emotional. He despised the birthright, then blamed Jacob. vowed murder in his rage. used women in retaliation. played "victim" when convenient. Esau's behavior taught Jacob early that *"People will rewrite history to suit their emotions."*

Laban's manipulation was more charming and could probably sell ice to an Ice Man. When Jacob reaches Laban's house, he arrives at the source of the family's manipulative culture.

Laban is Bethuel's legacy magnified the following which Laban had rehearsed to perfection, no doubt. Laban was welcoming, charming, flattering and at the same time, calculating, exploitative, contract shifting, but if you called him out on any of this, he could as easily induce you to feeling guilty for accusing him of such. Family doesn't treat family like this. We're close, right? We're family. We're blood.

I've heard it said on one, "That man? He'd sell his grandmother for a dollar. That was a ral life description of a Laban.

Jacob runs to Uncle Laban for protection, but he doesn't protect Jacob, he profits off Jacob, becoming Jacob's greatest earthly antagonist.

Jacob learned survival, not sincerity. Jacob's name means *"he grasps the heel; supplanter."* But this identity was not simply innate — it was also incubated. He wasn't simply born this way, he was by nurture created to be this way. He grew up around his mother's plots, Esau's emotional volatility. Although Bethuel's bargaining culture was in his blood, it wasn't fully brought out until he spent time with Uncle Laban. …Jacob became an adaptation of the home that formed him.

Through his mother Jacob learned that blessing had to be fought for—even stolen. Even by trickery if necessary. In Bethuel's culture nothing came free and even what you worked for and earned wasn't really yours. Nothing came easily. nothing came without negotiation. Therefore, Jacob learned in that culture that he had to also strategize—even out think the other strategists. He had to learn to anticipate, sharpen his deceiving gene, to maneuver and out maneuver those who were maneuvering against you. he had to learn to protect what's his, what he wants, and what he works for.

An upset mom of a toddler who has just heard foul words out of her child's mouth may ask, Where did you learn to talk like that? The kid will just look at the mom and say, I learned it from dad." (However we know not only dads need to check their language and adjective usage.)

Jacob became what his environment required. Many a man may ask a wife or girlfriend, "You were never like this. Where did you learn to be like this, or to talk like this."

Sadly, her answer often is, "I learned it from you."

Jacob became the best student of the system of House of Bethuel at Padam-Aram.

Like a low-level criminal going to jail, when he gets there, there are more like him and even more worse than he is--. Jacob learned how to be more like he was on his uncle's ranch.

Jacob became caught between TWO master manipulators. First, his mother's manipulation shaped him. Then Laban's manipulation refined him.

Between Rebekah and Laban, Jacob learned how to go along to get along. Laban had something he wanted: Rachel. Then later, when Laban wouldn't give Jacob any cattle, he had to create his own. All this time Jacob became sharper, tougher, wiser and more discerning.

Laban became the mirror God used to break Jacob's manipulative nature.

Jacob spent 20 years in Laban's house and during that time God allowed his transformation under much pressure. Changing salaries, exploitation, emotional pressure and possibly physical pressure also—he wanted Rachel but couldn't yet have her.

Why so long? Transformation conversion takes time. First, we have to yield to God, yield and submit to the process, and then the process can fully begin.

Jacob entered Laban's house as a supplanter. He left as a fighter for his own blessing. Later, he wrestled God as a broken man. He stood as Israel — a prince.

God, who can use foolish things to confound the wise, used master manipulators to strip manipulation out of Jacob.

LIVING WITH MASTER MANIPULATORS

A breakthrough teaching on how God uses difficult people to develop destiny. It will be a hard lesson and certainly unforgettable, but sometimes the manipulator can teach mor than the mentor.

The manipulators surrounding Jacob were his mother, Rebekah. She is the strategic manipulator (Loving, Protective, Calculated). Rebekah manipulates: Isaac, Esau, Jacob, the household rhythm, timing, emotions, outcomes. But we notice she never tried to manipulate her brother Laban or her father, Bethuel – her father's house.

Her love for Jacob was genuine, but her strategy was relentless. Using manipulation as protection, Rebekah's message to Jacob's soul: "You must outthink your enemies, even if they are your family."

There are seasons when God sends mentors. But there are also seasons when God allows manipulators — not to destroy you, but to develop you.

What a mentor teaches gently, a manipulator forces out of you. Mentors train you through guidance. Manipulators train you through pressure. Jacob learned strategy, stewardship, negotiation, discernment, emotional intelligence, boundary-setting, spiritual alertness, A manipulator will pull strength out of you that a gentle mentor may never trigger. Sometimes pressure activates potential.

Manipulators reveal what's hidden in you

Jacob had good things in him such as promise, blessing, anointing, and leadership, but he didn't *know* it yet. Laban's exploitation brought out Jacob's resilience, his creativity (spotted & speckled method), his determination, his spiritual sensitivity. Laban became the mirror that revealed Jacob's maturity.

A difficult person can sometimes show you more about yourself than a supportive one.

Manipulators expose the weaknesses you didn't know you had, not to shame you, but to strengthen you. Jacob learned patience under provocation, integrity under injustice, emotional regulation under pressure, wisdom in conversation, and discernment in relationships, even with relatives, elders, close relatives and people that you believe your parents have already vetted.

The manipulative environment was revealed where he needed refinement. God used discomfort as a diagnostic tool for Jacob.

Manipulators push you toward the presence of God. Jacob learned to depend on God because Laban was undependable. The more Laban shifted, the more Jacob sought God for direction. A manipulator indirectly forces you into deeper prayer, deeper, listening, deeper trust, and deeper revelation. Some people push you into destiny by pushing you to God.

Manipulators make you value what you once took for granted. Jacob grew up in Isaac's house — a place of blessing, inheritance, and stability. He didn't value those things until he lived under the wrong man. Isaac is a man who as a teenage was tied to an altar, you can't tell me that didn't affect the boy. That taught silent obedience. Period.

On the other hand, with Laban, manipulators teach what peace feels like by removing it. They show what honor looks like by withholding it. They define what truth is by flooding you with lies. They make you appreciate what freedom is by restricting it, and what dignity is by disrespecting it.

Pain of all kinds teaches appreciation but not in a perverse way.

Manipulators Make You Build Skills You Didn't Plan to Need. Jacob learned animal breeding not for a job, but for deliverance. Skills gained in survival seasons become keys in elevation seasons. One may learn financial Wisdom under a stingy boss. Emotional resilience under a critical parent. Negotiation under a controlling partner. Patience under a chaotic coworker, and boundaries under a narcissistic friend. Your discomfort is your education. Don't seek out uncomfortable situations, let the Lord send or place you where you should be.

Manipulators can unmask your divine assignment. Jacob came to Laban's house for survival, but he left with a lineage, a nation's foundation, newfound Wisdom, wealth. And on the way to where he was going, Jacob also acquired his new identity (Israel), a covenant destiny, and spiritual authority.

Uncle Laban, the manipulator, became the catalyst for transformation. Laban raised Jacob into Israel without knowing he was doing it. Your oppressor can't stop your destiny — they can accidentally prepare you for it.

God never lets a manipulator have the final say. God can use a person, a tribe, even a nation for something that seems uncomfortable or even punishing, but eventually if one of God's was hurt, that punisher will be punished. Laban tried to limit Jacob, but God gave Jacob visions, multiplied Jacob's flocks, protected Jacob in dreams, warned Laban not to harm Jacob, timed Jacob's exit, and put a boundary between them. The manipulator sharpened Jacob, but God established *Israel*. Manipulators shape you. But God seals you.

You graduate from manipulators — you don't stay with them. The lesson is temporary. The pain is temporary. The environment is temporary. When the training is over, God delivers you with evidence. Jacob left with wealth, strategy, unity (Rachel & Leah), clarity, identity, protection, revelation, and heirs.

What mentors teach by instruction, manipulators teach by opposition. One trains you by building. The other trains you by breaking and God uses both. A manipulator may have been a part of your story, but never part of your destiny. They were the pressure. God is the purpose. You survived the lesson and now you will rise into your calling.

Jacob lived his entire life between a mother who manipulated to protect him, and an uncle who manipulated to exploit him. Rebekah's household. Bethuel's household was the birthplace of this entire pattern. Jacob inherited their brilliance, their cunning, their instincts, their quick minds and strategic soul.

But God transformed those traits into leadership, discernment, spiritual authority, covenant identity, and the wisdom of a patriarch.

Between Rebekah and Laban, Jacob was broken. But with God, by God, and because of God, Jacob was rebuilt.

Isaac forged Jacob spiritually, but the Lord taught Jacob how to stand and how to fight because Laban was not just an uncle, he was an opponent. Isaac was an obedient soul and that is what he taught and imparted to Jacob, but Jacob needed more – he had 12 sons to raise where Isaac only had the two. And, it seemed that Rebekah had her hands all in it.

Through each of the manipulators and oppressors that we are looking at in this book, you could learn so much. Laban teaches boundaries, discernment, self-worth, identity, and strategy.

Pharaoh teaches warfare, deliverance, endurance, reliance on God, and the power of covenant.

Saul teaches how to carry yourself when wrongly accused, how to honor without being controlled, how to wait on God's timing, how to stay humble under attack, and how to succeed quietly.

JACOB'S SPIRITUAL LEGACY

Let's be real, up to this point, Jacob's entire life is marked by striving, conflict, and outmaneuvering people who should have loved him.

Where did he learn *that* pattern? First: from Esau drama. But lets talk about Rebekah and Laban's family of origin, Jacob learned this behavior from her mother, Laban's sister, and Laban is just like Rebekah. Trickster. Deceiver. Liar, basically. And Jacob whose name means, *supplanter* fits right in.

Then: Laban intensified it. This is no different than sending a criminal to jail, won't they, without God, just intensify their criminal behavior when they get around other criminals?

Laban became Jacob's authority, employer, and father for a season. He became Jacob's mirror and Jacob's disciplinarian. Laban became Jacob's reminder of his own trickster tendencies. Laban sharpened Jacob through suffering.

As one can put a thousand to flight and two--, ten thousand, the goal in the spirit is to tie or place two together for more power. That is a spiritual law and God is not the only one who desires that two be united as one--, it is for purpose and power and procreation.

Jacob going to Laban's ranch probably made the devil very happy. But it would be up to God to turn it to good for Jacob, for Isarel and ultimately for us.

LABAN STYLE

Laban ruled by fostering an environment of fear and walking on eggshells. He drained people in a pharaonic style so they couldn't afford to leave. Jacob fled secretly because he knew that "If Laban knew I wanted to leave, he'd take everything back by force." When you can't even say "bye"... When you have to run in the night... When telling the truth is dangerous That's the mark of a controlling household.

The controller plays the *victim;* the moment they lose control they were start playing vctim. This is another form of manipulation and control. If the controller can get you on the defensive, then you are easier to manipulate to prove that you're innocent, to prove that you did no wrong, to prove that you love them, to prove that you are ***not like that.***

Classic narcissistic move.

When Jacob finally left, Laban shows up shouting, "Why did you trick me?" as if Laban suddenly knew nothing about trickery. This is very much akin to Jacob tricking Esau and then running like a coward as if Esau was about to do him wrong. All the ways of a man are clean in his own eyes. Without Holy Spirit conviction, without the Law being preached to us, would any of us ever know that what we just did wasn't "clean"? When we are nose blind and can't smell our own funk, that is a sign that we all need the Holy Ghost and one-another ministry. Amen.

Jacob had the spirit of the trickster already and it was strengthened by being with Laban – he was just like his uncle, because his dad, Isaac wasn't anything like this. Isaac was an obedient sort, I'm sure of it. After Abraham tied him to that altar when he was just a teenager, I am sure Isaac did whatever his father said from then on. Period.

Yet, Laban would continue to complain against Jacob saying, "You stole my daughters!" I think he cared more about what he said next than what he first said. Then Laban said, "You took my idols!" Think of how odd that is since Laban knew that Jacob served the Only Living God so Jacob would have no need of idols. Yet, Uncle Laban accused his nephew-son-in-law, Jacob.

The manipulative sort has a few tools in his arsenal, and he knows either how to use them and in what order. Or, he just throws out what he thinks will work. Next, Laban shifted into self-pity and performative outrage.

Spiritually, Laban's behavior created generational effects. Here's the uncomfortable truth: Laban's manipulation didn't end with him. It rippled into: Rachel and Leah's children.

The birth order drama not just of that family, but throughout the Bible. Joseph and his brothers' jealousy. Family patterns of deception.

Household *gods*, hidden loyalties, and spiritual confusion. Divination leads to Idolatry and Idolatry leads to the afflictions of barrenness, poverty, and slavery. There it is--, in that family. Laban planted seeds that the next generations fought through.

So yes — Laban didn't just wrong Jacob. He disrupted an entire *community* of people around him.

He was: A master manipulator. A financial abuser. A deceptive patriarch. A father who failed his daughters. A spiritual contaminator. A man whose influence outlived him and the spirit of Laban is alive today. This is why this book has been written to inform and for deliverance from that spirit and it's effects over your life. In the Name of Jesus. Amen.

WHAT ABOUT YOU?

Where are you now? What about you? Are you under a Laban spirit? Have you been trapped or worse, captured by someone with the spirit of Laban? As we are seeing, there are Laban's in families. There are Laban employers, Laban bosses. The spirit of Laban is pervasive it could be in any willing or unsuspecting, dry, un-prayed up soul. It could be in a greedy, covetous, prideful sort. It could even be in a church—even in the leadership.

Laban's actions didn't just create relational drama — they set off spiritual repercussions that affected generations. His behavior opened doors to oppression, strife, and confusion.

Laban operated in deception, and deception breeds disorder. He tricked Jacob with Leah. He manipulated wages. He misled his daughters. He did it all. Where deception is present, there is: confusion, mistrust, rivalry, spiritual instability, (Compare James 3:16: *"Where envy and strife is, there is confusion and every evil work."*)

He used people as tools — opening the door to generational trauma. God values people. Laban valued leverage. When someone treats others as commodities, it strips their dignity. It confuses and damages their identity. If you don't know who you are, you risk being out of authority and dominion, and your destiny is at risk. It creates insecurity and the trauma of it becomes hereditary.

The rivalry of Rachel & Leah led to the jealousy among Jacob's sons. Which lead to Joseph's brothers turning on him, and that all traces back to familial patterns. Laban.

He held idols in his household and God hates idolatry. Rachel stole Laban's "teraphim" because they represented inheritance rights, spiritual authority, and household gods. Laban was not walking with Israel's God. His house was a house of mixture, and mixture produces spiritual confusion, divided loyalty, hidden bondage, the curses attached to idolatry.

He practiced control, opening the door to oppression. That's no surprise if he's practicing divination… control, domination, oppression, witchcraft—that all accompanies it.

Control is a counterfeit of God's leadership. Laban didn't lead; he dominated. Oppression breeds fear, silence, flight, emotional captivity.

His manipulation created a spiritual atmosphere of rivalry and barrenness. Notice: Rachel struggled with barrenness in Laban's house. Once freed, fruitfulness began to manifest. Spiritually Manipulative environments lead to barrenness, choking fertility — natural, emotional, spiritual, and financial.

Laban fits multiple traits seen in modern behavioral psychology. He had **narcissistic traits leading to a s**ense of entitlement. Exploiting others without conscience. A lack of empathy. Blame shifter when confronted. Shifts to victimhood when being found out or losing control. Laban is the **covert manipulator who will s**mile-in-your-face tactics. Changes rules midstream—whatever gives them the most advantage. Uses guilt, obligation, and tradition as tools. Controls by ambiguity (changing wages "ten times"). Laban is the **financial abuser - Uses** money to entice or trap others. Withholds wages creates and enforces dependency. Never intends to release those he profits from.

Laban is know for emotional neglect and instrumental parenting. His daughters proved it when they said, "He has sold us." Meaning he objectified us and didn't treat us like people, and especially not like daughters.

He is the strategic opportunist who only seeks to benefit himself, extend his control, and advance his agenda. Laban was territorial – he believed he owned people: Laban chased Jacob because he believed he "owned."

Jacob, his own daughters, the grandchildren, the herds of cattle, the flocks of sheep, the future. Classic territorial spirit attached to narcissism and idolatry.

LABAN VS. JACOB COMPARATIVE CHART

Category	Laban	Jacob
Motivation	Control & personal gain	Covenant, legacy, identity
Methods	Deception, manipulation	Strategy, perseverance
Leadership Style	Oppressive	Transformational (over time)
View of People	Tools & leverage	Family & inheritance
Spiritual Position	Idol worship & mixture	Chosen lineage of promise

Category	Laban	Jacob
Primary Weapon	Confusion	Faith & negotiation
Emotional Pattern	Blame shift & victimhood	Fear → courage through encounter with God
End Result	Loses everything he tried to control	Leaves with abundance
Relationship to God	None shown	Wrestles with God, transformed into Israel
Legacy	Chaos, division	Nation, covenant blessing

Laban adversely affects on his daughters and since he adversely affected Jacob and these women were married to Jacob, Laban had a double negative effect on his own grandchildren. For this and many other reasons, tis is why people of the same household shouldn't marry. They are increasing negativity exponentially and that is very dangerous as well as negative DNA consequences and foremost because it is illegal in the natural and Leviticus says don't do it.

Leah was thrust into marriage by deception. She ended up feeling unloved by Jacob as well as undervalued by her own father. She spent her life trying to earn affection. She suffered with rejection and comparison-it is to her co-wife—her sister, Rachel. Ultimately, Leah's identity became tied to her ability to have children.

Laban planted the insecurity that defined her.

Rachel suffered even more profoundly than Leah. She suffered emotional abandonment. Her father did not protect her. He *deliberately* subjected her to an unfair marriage structure. Rachel learned early that her feelings didn't really matter to her father. And that her father would even sacrifice her sister, or her for his own agenda.

Forced into rivalry. Rachel didn't choose competition with Leah; Laban engineered it. Polygamous marriage always have the following but being married to the same man as your sister had to be grievous. In that household there was jealousy, striving, desperation for validation, and comparison-itis.

Rachel had to be spiritually confused due to Laban's idols. Rachel grew up in a spiritually mixed home. Her attachment to the teraphim shows her insecurity around inheritance--, really both she and her sister suffered this insecurity. Rachel seems to have been in some kind of mixture of religion with blurred spiritual boundaries

Barrenness arrived in Laban's environment mostly for spiritual reasons because of the divination and the idolatry. But if we look very closely we will see that as barrenness is hitting Laban's livestock that is symbolic of what is happening in the spirit realm. Jacob's cattle, formerly not the most prevalent versions were multiplying very well, and Laban whose cattle was the predominant breed and brand were much fewer in number over the six years. This is God. This is judgment. This is an echo or a shadow of the barrenness that would reach Laban's house, starting with Rachel.

Barrenness in Scripture often symbolizes emotional blockage, spiritual oppression and generational curses.

Once away from Laban's household, God "remembered Rachel." When there is barrenness and it is not broken or removed by God, then the only way to prosper in anything, whether in business or fruit of the womb is to have someone to do it for you, or take it from someone. Laban's house suffered barrenness in Rachel, but not in Leah. It does not say so in the Bible, but that makes me wonder if Laban had possibly dedicated Rachel. It could explain why he didn't let her go in the first place, but let Leah go. Sure, Leah was older and the custom was that the older daughter marries first, but Laban was reticent to let Rachel go into marriage with Jacob.

Rachel died young, giving birth to Benjamin. Some believe the lingering effects of family dysfunction, rivalry, and spiritual mixture contributed to the atmosphere around her life.

Didn't it benefit Laban to keep Rachel unmarried? Yes, it kept Jacob working and possibly distracted, since we know that Laban changed Jacob's wages ten times.

SPOTTING LABAN-TYPES

How to Recognize Modern-Day manipulators Hiding Behind Niceness

A Laban-type is not always loud, violent, or openly wicked. Most times, they're *subtle*, pleasant, and even "helpful. "But underneath the smile is a strategic agenda designed to benefit them while trapping you. Below are the signatures — the red flags — of a Laban-type person.

They are flakey, flippant and often will change the agreement after you commit. Laban promised Rachel, but delivered Leah. He promised wages but changed them "ten times" as Jacob had said.

Modern signs are: They promise one thing, then "renegotiate" after you've already invested. They shift expectations to keep you off balance. They create rules that only benefit *them*. Their goal is to keep you tied to them through confusion.

Like a slaveowner, only nicer--they never intend to release you. Take note, Laban types work in environments of near-equality or seeming equality. This is not the slave to master relationships. Laban is adept in making his victim feel seen, noticed, appreciated, and even respected. That is part of the game this *spirit* plays. Many years ago I was offered a work position by an employer that I admired. The pay offer was approximately one half of the going rate. I respectfully declined. Had I accepted that job, I may have been signing with a Laban-type.

Jacob worked 20 years. Every blessing Jacob generated, Laban tried to tie to himself and keep for himself. Now, if Laban's idol or idols were all that, then wouldn't he have a hunk of money and not have to trick others to work for him while he ripped them off? But perhaps Laban used the idols to confuse his "workers" so he could steal from them.

Modern signs that you are dealing with a Laban spirit: They guilt you when you try to step back. They get angry or offended when you set boundaries. They act like your growth is a betrayal. They never celebrate your independence — only your dependence. Their goal is control disguised as "connection."

The Laban spirit uses people as tools, as means to an end they want to reach. Laban didn't even protect his daughters — he leveraged them. They are the type who love you as long as you are doing what they want you to do, or doing something that benefits them. They "love" you when you are useful, they ignore or diminish you when you're not. To them, connections and relationships are transactions. People are pawns in their strategy.

They play the victim and guilt trip you when you finally speak up. Jacob finally left Laban, quietly; Laban shows up shouting: "You stole from me!" — when Laban was the thief. That spirit will make whomever it possesses cry, pout, or rage when confronted. They act like *you* are the problem. They pretend to be wounded while hiding their own wrongdoing. They twist the story, so you feel guilty for standing up for yourself. Their goal is to regain control through emotional manipulation.

They create environments of jealousy, rivalry, or comparison. Rachel and Leah's rivalry was engineered by Laban's deception. They pit people against each other. They stir up competition to keep you from uniting. They "triangulate" (telling each person a different story). They create confusion so you don't notice their manipulation. Their goal is to divide and rule.

Even when they are wrong and they get caught in their mischief, they will double down, triple down, never admitting that they are wrong. Laban ransacked Jacob's tents, found no proof of his accusations against Jacob and **STILL** didn't apologize. That Laban spirit will deflect, distract, or deny. They will shift the blame, throwing anyone under the bus— every time.

'What had happened was--- they rewrite the story to preserve their image—they are not foreign to lying. They justify every action, no matter how harmful. Their goal is to maintain their false righteousness. They are possessive, but will have you thinking they are protective, so you let down your discernment and your guard.

Laban chased Jacob as if he *owned* him—feeling entitled to Jacob's time, energy, and work. He behaved as if Jacob's blessings belong to Laban. He was possessive and territorial toward Jacob. They will desperately try to keep you from other opportunities, connections and other people. They want you to need them and look only to them. Their game is to give you a little, maybe just enough, or almost enough, but never all that you are due and never all that you are capable to achieving.

They flatter publicly, but control privately. Each time you may be thinking or hoping, oh, they've changed now. Now I will be respected. Didn't this happen to Leah four times with Jacob as her husband? I'm not saying that Jacob had Laban's spirit, I'm saying Leah's reaction and response to normal life was programmed by Laban, her father. If I try harder, if I do this, If I do more, if I keep up and be consistent. And to the embattled woman might say, if I love him more, if I show him that I love him more, then he will change.

The *Laban spirit* does not change. Period. You can't change it; you must get rid of it.

Laban called Jacob "my bone and my flesh" — while exploiting him. An abusive spouse my call their spouse, Honey, Babe, and my love in public and still be abusive in private. Modern signs are just that: public praise, private manipulation. They may say, "You're like family to me!" and then follow it up with unreasonable demands. They appear kind to outsiders while draining you silently. Their public image is important to them: People think they are the greatest, but you know better. The only reason this spirit has any staying power is that its victim believes the public persona more than they see, believe, and discern the truth. The other reason that it lasts is because it has drained its victims of means, physical, financial means to leave the relationship or the location.

Their goal is to keep the victim dependent, especially financial dependence. Jacob's entire livelihood was tied to Laban for 20 years. It was the same as being tied down. The Laban type employer will hold back opportunities, they underpay, overwork, or "forget" agreements or promises, such as your pay increase, your bonuses or commissions. They create situations where you *need* them financially. The worst of them use witchcraft to accomplish all this--, creating the problem and hoping that you will reach out to them for the solution. That's the devil's game.

They make you believe you can't succeed without them. Their goal is to secure their power through your need.

Those who carry the Laban spirit are spiritually mixed or compromised in their faith.

Laban carried idols while claiming loyalty to Jacob's God. They use Bible verses, even God-talk, but they are far from it. They operate in confusion, jealousy, and hidden agendas, many times hiding behind the Word of God, especially if he is distorting that Word. Their goal is to plow with God's heifer; to use spirituality as a tool, not as truth.

They resent your breakthrough. The moment Jacob prospered, Laban's sons became jealous. You can improve, you can work harder, but you had better not surpass them. Those with this spirit will downplay your blessings. They act irritated or threatened when God opens doors for you and will discourage you from going through open doors that God has created for you. Careful who you tell your dreams and plans to because if they have your ear, they may talk you out of what God has prepared for you.

Worse, they are backbiters, they talk about you behind your back when you advance. their goal is to keep you smaller than them, under them, and helping them to be enriched.

They make you feel like you owe them your life. Even after Jacob's decades of labor, Laban said, "These daughters are *mine*. These flocks are *mine*." After all I've done for you… You've heard these phrases, I'm sure. They exaggerate what they've done for you. They weaponize "loyalty." They claim ownership over your progress. They make you feel ungrateful for wanting peace. Their goal is to bind you with false obligation.

THE BIG TEST

How to know you're dealing with a Laban-type. Ask yourself:

Does this person benefit more from me staying stuck than from me being free? If the answer is yes, you are dealing with a Laban.

LABAN vs PHARAOH vs SAUL

Laban, Pharaoh, and Saul: three Different Spirits of Bondage, Three Different Types of Manipulators

These three men represent three distinct patterns of oppression you'll see in Scripture *and in life*. The differences matter — because each one traps people in a different way, and each one requires a different kind of spiritual response.

Let's differentiate them by looking at several things, first their primary method of control.

Laban uses manipulative control. He smiles in your face. He shifts agreements. He uses guilt, obligation, and emotional leverage. He exploits relationships. He changes the terms whenever you get ahead. He can look you right in the face, while draining you. His weapon is manipulation, and manipulation is witchcraft.

Pharaoh is very powerful and uses oppressive control. Openly dominates. He enforces heavy burdens. He uses fear and physical intimidation. He doesn't use charm, he uses threats and cruelty. Demands endless productivity. Punishes freedom. He tries to kill legacy (Hebrew sons). His weapon is force.

And then there's Saul who uses jealous control. He loves you until he fears you. He is more spiritual in that he sabotages your calling. The Saul spirit throws spears when you shine. Wants your gift but not your growth. He seems spiritual on the outside, but he is emotionally unstable. He is obsessed with keeping the throne and he may see you as a threat. If you are, you instantly become a target. He cannot stand being overshadowed. His weapon is jealousy-driven sabotage.

When it comes to God and Godliness, Laban is spiritually mixed. He has household idols. He uses God's name selectively and has no real fear of God. To Laban, spirituality is just a tool.

When it comes to God and the things of God, Pharaoh is a defiant atheist. "Who is the Lord that I should obey Him?" Pharaoh is hard-hearted and rejects God repeatedly. Pharaoh believes that he is a *god*. He will even battle God openly.

When it comes to God, Saul may start out okay but may end up in rebellion. The Spirit of God will depart from him. Saul will use religion to look obedient while disobeying God. He consults a medium in desperation, thereby mixing religions making him akin to Laban. Of the three, they all reject God in some way. Saul, more than the others represents fallen leadership because at least he did start out with God.

Laban's reaction to your growth Is that he becomes *threatened and deceptive*. His sons become jealous and Laban tries to keep Jacob small. Your growth will expose Laban's insecurity.

Pharaoh, in comparison, when Israel grows, he increases oppression and violence. He tries to crush their multiplication. Your growth makes him escalate attacks.

Saul saw David succeed and lost control emotionally. Akin to Laban, Saul will praise you in public but plots in private.

Your growth triggers his insecurity, paranoia, and anger. Laban will take your time wages, energy, identity, clarity, emotional peace, and family unity. Laban is the emptier. Jacob said, "You would have sent me away empty. Leah and Rachel felt that their father had taken all from them. Laban steals slowly, quietly, and gradually.

Pharaoh takes freedom, labor, generational destiny, human dignity, and spiritual stamina. Pharaoh steals openly and brutally.

Saul's method includes the taking of opportunities, recognition, safety, emotional stability, and peace of mind. Saul steals spiritually and psychologically, through sabotage.

Laban fears losing control of another's productivity the most. Pharaoh fears losing control of another's body and labor. Saul fears losing control of the throne and the spotlight. Their eventual downfall Laban was outwitted by Jacob, restrained by God in a dream, forced into peace. Pharaoh was destroyed in the Red Sea, judged for stubborn rebellion. Saul dies by his own sword after years of spiritual decline and jealousy.

Today, Laban is the Narcissistic Manipulator. You can see this *spirit* in family members who guilt you, bosses who underpay you, Parents who emotionally control you, leaders who use you then blame you, and in people who want loyalty but offer you none.

You can see the *spirit of pharaoh* in the abusive oppressors, toxic workplaces, systemic oppression, controlling organizations, in leaders who use fear to dominate, and in environments that crush identity.

Saul *spirit* is that of the jealous saboteur. It is seen in leaders threatened by your gifting, friends who become competitors—even boyfriends, girlfriends and spouses who compete with you for no real reason. You can see this spirit in mentors who turn into enemies, p, and in people who love you until you succeed, and in spiritual authority figures who can't handle your anointing.

WHEN YOUR BLESSING IS IN THE HOUSE OF LABAN

When you know that you are blessed by God, but stuck under someone else's control, you need the Lord more than ever. If you are growing, but growing in the wrong house, favored, but exploited by the environment—God is the only one to call on. *God can hide favor in uncomfortable places to grow you, refine you, and position you for release.* All hostile environments are survival mode; yet God will sometimes allow growth in a hostile environment. Jacob's blessing didn't *start* when he left Laban, it started inside Laban's house. Jacob found his wife there, built his family there, gained wealth there, gained Wisdom there, discovered God's faithfulness there.

Why?

Because Jacob needed *pressure* to transform. God often hides blessing in places where your character must rise to the challenge.

Know this: *You can be divinely blessed while living under human oppression.* Not every uncomfortable environment is demonic; some are developmental. God will let a manipulator reveal your identity. Jacob was always blessed, but he didn't see the magnitude of the blessing until Laban tried to cap it.

A Laban-type person forces you to discover your own strength, your capacity and your gifting. It forces you to use your discernment, resilience, and value. This kind of pressure forces revelation. Jacob learned who he truly was because Laban tricked him more than once and tried to shrink him. Imagine Jacob's growth when he found out that if he was a bully there was one bigger than himself. Imagine knowing that he is a trickster, but he now was dependent up the master of trickery, Uncle Laban.

Sometimes, the very person trying to limit you is the one who accidentally activates your power.

What God has for you; it is for you. Even though your blessing gets delayed, it cannot be denied. Believe that. Laban in all of his trickery and tomfoolery delayed Jacob's blessing quite a bit by, tricking him, underpaying him, changing wages, trapping him, and keeping him poor, making Jacob dependent and needing to stay at Laban's ranch.

Yet Laban knew that because of Jacob's presence, that is why his ranch was prospering. Where the presence of God is there is prosperity. Laban believed in that to some extent: he thought that the presence of idols would prosper him, but it was Jacob's presence that blessed him. And since he was ripping Jacob off, this was like an evil exchange as Laban used his nephew.

But God overruled every tactic. Jacob said:

"God did not allow him to harm me." (Gen. 31:7) When God's hand is on you, manipulation may delay, but it cannot stop manifestation. What's yours is inevitably, eventually, and undeniably yours.

Inside Laban's house, Jacob learned animal husbandry, agriculture, livestock management, wealth creation, negotiation, spiritual listening, endurance. He would learn responsibility, patience, long-suffering, and also leadership. He also learned who he was by looking in the mirror of his character flaws that were loudly shown in Laban. To his good, Jacob was developing skills required to steward a nation. Jacob walked into Laban's house as one man. He left as the head of Israel.

The training ground was unfair, hard, maybe even harsh, but it was effective. Sometimes your blessing is hidden in labor, not in luxury. Laban's house wasn't glamorous. Ranching is hard work. Jacob slept outside. He worked in heat and cold. He endured injustice, lived in tension, also knowing that if he left, his brother Esau is somewhere out there waiting to kill him.

Yet in that space, God revealed strategies. God revealed visions (the speckled & spotted method). God revealed protection. God revealed abundance.

The place you hate can become the place God visits you if you are diligent, don't murmur and complain and serve with dedication and honor. If the Lord finds you working and occupying, He can use that and He can bless you right there as you are growing, developing and being refined in the fires of life.

The conditions of Laban's House will force you to value freedom. If Jacob had stayed with his family (Isaac's house), he might never have valued his autonomy, boundaries, spiritual authority, personal identity, family unity, and generational legacy. Freedom means more--, it means everything after you've tasted captivity.

While Jacob was sustained, or semi-sustained at Laban's--, well, at least he wasn't dead, Esau didn't break into the ranch and kill Jacob.

At one point God said, "Return to the land of your fathers." (Gen 31:3). Translated, that meant that God was saying something like, You're done learning. You're done surviving. You're done enduring. You're done building someone else's empire. It's time to be established on your own terms.

A Laban-house is a place to pass through — not a place to settle—like a place of tents. The blessing there may be real, but it is temporal not permanent.

Jacob arrived at Laban's house with *nothing*.

He left with two wives, two handmaidens, children, servants, livestock, wealth, influence, spiritual authority, and destiny clarity. Jacob still had the birthright that he stole from Esau, and this could be why all these blessings were attracted to Jacob.

Laban was an idolater who tried to steal from a child of God, therefore, Laban lost what Jacob gained. Manipulators always lose more than they steal.

By Prophecy: God Times Your Breakout So even Laban can't stop it.

1. In the Name of Jesus, Father, although the blessings you have for me may tarry, let them come to me in Your perfect time. Lord, prepare me, and expedite the time, in the Name of Jesus.

Jacob didn't leave by luck; he left by instruction. When you have a Word from God, yu have anointing, you have divine escort—no one and nothing can stop you. God waited until Laban's sons were distracted and Laban's favor had shifted. He waited until Jacob was spiritually strong and after Rachel & Leah saw the truth and supported Jacob.

Only then did God say, "Now rise and go." God will not let you leave until you can leave clean. Some exits require timing and strategy. Some require revelation. Many require unity and protection.

We all pray to God for breakthrough, but breakout is never random.

God will make your blessing untouchable.. You should stop and pray that prayer now:

1. **Father, in the Name of Jesus, make my blessings untouchable by any enemy, manipulator, or fake friend.**

When Laban tried to chase Jacob down, God warned him in a dream:

> Be careful that you do not say anything to Jacob, good or bad. (Genesis 31:24)

This means, "Do NOT speak curses. Do NOT manipulate. Do NOT interfere." God Himself defended Jacob's blessing. What God protects, no Laban can reclaim. Leaving Laban requires a boundary line. Jacob and Laban built Mizpah, which was a boundary line. **"May God watch between us… neither of us will cross this line to harm the other."** This wasn't a friendship prayer; to me it was like a restraining-order-in-stone.

PRAYER FOR DISCERNING THE SEASON OF RELEASE

(When you're not sure if you're supposed to endure, confront, or exit, this prayer will help.)

Father, in the Name of Jesus,
I come before You asking for clarity, Wisdom, and spiritual discernment.
You are the God who orders my steps,
the Shepherd who leads me,
and the Author of my times and seasons.

Lord, open my eyes to see Your timing, not my emotion. Open my ears to hear Your instruction, not my fear. Open my spirit to sense Your leading, not pressure or guilt.

If I am meant to stay, give me grace to endure, wisdom to navigate, and favor that preserves my peace.

If I am meant to go, give me courage to obey, strategy to move, and supernatural protection as I transition.

Reveal the true condition of the environment I am in. Expose motives, intentions, and the spiritual atmosphere.
Let me not be deceived by appearances, nor misled by flattery, familiarity, or false obligation.

Lord, show me clearly when a relationship has expired, when a season has closed, when an assignment is complete, when a door is no longer mine, when a blessing has finished maturing, when it is time to rise and return to what You prepared.

Just as You spoke to Jacob, speak to me with clarity. Whether through dreams, Scripture, conviction, or divine alignment — make the path unmistakable.

Give me boldness to obey quickly and humility to move quietly. Set boundaries where necessary, and send provision where needed.

Father, protect me from premature exits and from prolonged captivity. Place me squarely in Your timing.

Seal me in Your will. Guard me in Your timing. Guide me in Your peace.

I receive clarity now. I receive direction now. I receive peace now.

I receive the power and the authority to proclaim an end to a season when You say it is over, in the Name of Jesus. Amen.

GOD-LED BREAKAWAYS

How God delivers His people without noise, drama, or apology.

There is a pattern in Scripture that few people talk about, yet it is one of the most consistent ways God rescues His people. God can deliver quietly, and He often does. He sent His Word and healed them is deliverance. God often moves people silently. God often leads breakaways with strategy, not spectacle. Jacob left Laban quietly. Moses fled Pharaoh quietly. David escaped Saul quietly. Jesus slipped away from murderous crowds quietly.

The Kingdom of God is loud when it needs to be, but there is no reason to fear deliverance because often it is discreet. The Holy Spirit will never embarrass you and the Lord will not bring His people to shame. Sometimes full deliverance is just a Word. It could be a Word you read in your Bible. So read your Bible, there is health, healing, wealth, and wholeness in it.

God can deliver you in silence to protect you from retaliation. Jacob didn't leave Laban with a parade, but he did leave at the right moment, without announcement to Laban. Jacob left fully under God's direction, for his safety and the safety of his family-- Laban was the kind of man who would attempt to sabotage a public exit. Some exits must be quiet because the environment is unsafe.

God knows who will retaliate. God knows who will try to guilt you. God knows who will chase you to drag you back, or try to fight or harm you if you leave. (Pharaoh comes to mind.)

So, God leads you out in a whisper, not a shout.

Quiet exits prevent unnecessary explanation. Sometimes the moment you tell manipulative people you're leaving, they will bargain (or try to). They may cry, (or pretend to). They may try to guilt-trip you, lie, twist the narrative, The real narcissist will launch a smear campaign.

Neither God, nor Jacob gave Laban a chance to twist anything. Some people want drama, but quiet exits protect your clarity. There is no debate, no negotiation, no emotional tug-of-war--, just obedience. Sometimes the holy thing is to leave quietly and let God handle the commentary.

God will let you breakaway when the assignment is complete. FYI: That is true on the dark side too. In relationships that is why sometimes that person will ghost you. Poof! They are just gone because **their assignment against you is over.**

Assignment Over: Jacob served his time. His training season was done. His blessing had matured. His spirit was strengthened. His discernment was sharp. Then God said:

Return to the land of your fathers. (Gen. 31:3)

You may have heard it said that you can't leave a place until you love it. God's way is that you don't get to leave when you're irritated — you leave when you're released. A God-led exit has these characteristics: divine timing, divine protection, divine clarity, divine favor. Leaving is not on impulse; it is by instruction. You must wait until God *sends* you.

Quiet exits are biblical, not cowardly. You don't owe everyone an explanation. You don't have to "stay and tough it out" if God says you may leave. Know this: closure is spiritual, not just emotional.

Scripture repeatedly shows quiet departures as righteous strategy. David escaped Saul without a goodbye. Joseph and Mary escaped Herod's massacre in the night. Paul escaped Damascus through a basket. Jesus escaped hostile crowds by "slipping away." A quiet exit is not weakness. Spiritual stealth mode is a thing, after all. Leaving by a Word of Knowledge and with Wisdom under divine instruction and anointing is God's way.

God sometimes hides you to heal you. to save you. to keep you. if you can't heal in the same atmosphere that made you bleed. You can't recover in the same environment that drained you. Sometimes God leads you out quietly because He is rebuilding your identity, restoring your dignity, strengthening your voice, is renewing your confidence, and or resetting your boundaries.

Some breakthroughs happen in silence so they cannot be sabotaged. In the Old and New Testaments prophets, and even Jesus shut the door to onlookers when healing was going forth.

Quiet exits reveal people's true hearts. Notice what happened after Jacob left. Laban's sons suddenly accused him. Laban suddenly acted like the victim. The atmosphere shifted; there was clarity once Jacob stepped away. Sometimes your absence reveals more truth than your presence ever could.

A quiet exit is protective while it exposes motives, clarifies relationships, separates the loyal from the opportunistic, reveals who valued you vs who used you. Who they become when you leave is who they always were. God-led breakaways happen in moments, not months. that is why in the Old Testament the Passover meal is eaten in haste. long discussions and drawn-out explanations are rarely Spirit-led. Most divine breakaways happen fast:

- "Rise and go now."
- "Flee."
- "Depart quickly."
- "Leave this place."
- "Why sit we here until we die?"

God moves you when the timing is right (safe), the enemy is distracted (or down), the door is open, the atmosphere is ready. Timing is everything in spiritual escape. If God says, "Go!" the longer you wait, the tighter the trap becomes.

A quiet exit doesn't necessarily mean a quiet destiny. Jacob left silently… …but entered a destiny so loud it shook nations. David fled Saul quietly but became Israel's greatest king. Jesus slipped away from danger, but His resurrection shook the universe. Quiet exits often lead to loud destinies. Don't confuse a silent transition with a small future. Even when the silence is temporary — the impact is eternal.

Did anyone **see** the angel roll the stone back and Jesus leave the tomb that they had buried Him in? That was a quiet exit, but Jesus' ministry is still speaking.

God seals your breakaway with divine boundaries. After Jacob left, God Himself warned Laban in a dream:

"Do not say anything to Jacob, good or bad."

When God orchestrates a breakaway, the manipulator can't curse you, they can't interfere, they can't stop you, they can't touch what God protected. When Jacob and Laban finally met, they built a boundary line (Mizpah) that neither of them could cross. Every God-led breakaway ends with protection.

Quiet exits position you for what you couldn't receive where you were. Jacob couldn't become "Israel" in Laban's house. He had to leave the old environment to receive his new identity, a new encounter with God, a new blessing, a new legacy, and a new promise.

Some things God wants to give you can't come where you are. A quiet exit isn't just departure — it's positioning.

Your exit may be silent, but your deliverance is supernatural. Your transition may be quiet, but your destiny is loud. When God leads a breakaway, no Laban, no Pharaoh, no Saul, no idol, and no manipulative voice can follow you across the line He draws.

> And Jacob took a stone, and set it up for a pillar. And Jacob said unto his brethren, Gather stones; and they took stones, and made an heap: and they did eat there upon the heap.
>
> And Laban called it Jegarsahadutha: but Jacob called it Galeed. And Laban said, This heap is a witness

between me and thee this day. Therefore was the name of it called Galeed;

And Mizpah; for he said, The Lord watch between me and thee, when we are absent one from another. (Genesis 31:45-49)

They made what they called a covenant but it looked like a restraining order to me. A boundary, a line that each agreed not to cross ever again and they bought God into it. (vs 52-54)

This is what freedom looks like once escaping Laban: A quiet exit "in the night, clear boundaries (Mizpah line). God blocks retaliation and you leave with abundance.

Your identity transforms afterward (Jacob → Israel)

Breakthrough comes through clarity and boundaries.

Escaping Pharaoh looks like this: There is visible deliverance with signs. God breaks oppression openly. You leave with plunder. You also enter covenant identity. Freedom comes through divine intervention. Breakthrough comes through power and confrontation.

Escaping from Saul goes like this: God removes you before he kills you. You hide, wait, and develop. God raises you in secret. Deliverance comes through relocation and divine timing. Saul destroys himself. Breakthrough comes through distance and waiting on God's timing.

12 SIGNS GOD IS RELEASING YOU

How to recognize when your season has closed and your exit is ordained.

These signs come straight from Biblical patterns such as Jacob leaving Laban, David leaving Saul, Abraham leaving his homeland, Moses leaving Egypt, and Israel leaving bondage. When God is shifting your season, the signals are precise. The first thing you may notice is that the Grace to endure begins to lift. What you used to tolerate with patience now drains you. Grace is a power and if it is gone there is no anointing to continue in what you may have thought was normal, but now it is messiness or foolishness to you. When God ends a season, He removes the supernatural strength that kept you there.

When the Peace leaves, that's another sign. Even when nothing external is different, something internal could feel off, unsettled, unaligned, or restless. This is the Holy Spirit nudging your spirit into movement. God disturbs your comfort to reveal or remind you of your calling.

The environment no longer fits who you're becoming. God will grow you past an environment.

You may look around and realize that this situation doesn't match you anymore. The space feels small—too small for your growth. You may even feel that you are shrinking yourself to stay there. This is identity outgrowing captivity. And that is one of the main reasons that the devil doesn't want you to know who you are—your true identity because you would then rise up and walk out of any place he's trying to hold you.

You may notice that relationships in the environment shift unexpectedly. It could be that people suddenly withdraw, your favor changes, it's hard to have conversations with people. It could be that support dries up. Soon you may see that hidden motives are exposed. You may sense an increase in spiritual tension. Nothing is wrong; this could all be signs of a divine dislodging. God removes emotional glue so leaving no longer feels improbable or impossible.

Dreams, visions, or strong impressions will increase. **Pay attention.** God begins speaking more frequently through dreams, the Holy Spirit, Scripture prophetic voices and you may see repeated themes. God is preparing your spirit before He moves your feet.

God removes the fear of leaving. What terrified you last season no longer intimidates you. Where there was fear, hesitation or anxiety, God has replaced it with boldness, restlessness, resolve, or readiness. If fear is gone, the hand of God is near.

Provision for the move begins appearing in unexpected places. When God is releasing you, He starts shifting provision ahead of your departure. New opportunities, open doors, unexpected resources, or fresh ideas begin showing up — not where you are, but where you're *going*. Provision always moves before the person does. Kinda like manna moved with Israel through the Wilderness.

You feel internal release even before you make external moves. This can be subtle but powerful. Suddenly you get a knowing that you're done, that your assignment is complete, and that there is nothing else to learn here, as well, you may feel or know that there is nothing else for you to give or receive here. It's time to go. This is a spiritual release — not to be confused with emotional burnout.

The environment begins to push you out. **Bye Felicia!** Not always through conflict. Sometimes through discomfort, lack of fulfillment, stagnation, blocked progress, increased pressure, or even divine friction you realize that it is time o go. God uses holy discomfort to move you out of places you would never leave willingly. But that pressure is protection.

Conversations with God shift from 'stay' to 'go.' you get a knowing in your knower that it's time. In previous seasons, every time you prayed about leaving, God said, "Not yet" or "Wait." But now, the tone You start sensing is move, new direction, movement, transition, and release. Your spirit knows before your mind understands.

You start seeing signs of what's next. Before God moves you out, He reveals glimpses of the next season possibly showing you a new vision, a new assignment a new idea, a new opportunity, a new clarity, a new yearning. God never ends a season without preparing a new one.

God protects the exit and blocks retaliation; Hallelujah! Just like He warned Laban in a dream, God protects your transition. You may notice resistance falling flat, or the opposition silenced. Manipulative people may be losing influence. Attempts to control you weaken and people who held sway or power over you find that power breaking. This is divine shielding. When heaven guards the exit, hell can't close it.

When God releases you, the door doesn't slam, it simply stops opening. The environment stops feeding you. The peace stops resting on it. And the grace stops flowing there. That's when you know that you're being led into your next season.

Get out!

Now, after you're freed, you may begin to see a new you. Jacob became Israel after he left Laban. You gain identity, blessing, and generational purpose. After leaving Pharaoh the Hebrews became a nation. You gain freedom, covenant, and destiny. After leaving Saul, David became a king. Now, you step into God-given authority, maturity, and influence.

Laban binds you through manipulation. Pharaoh binds you through oppression. Saul binds you through jealousy. Laban shrinks you. Pharaoh crushes you. Saul sabotages you. But God delivers from all three and each deliverance upgrades your identity and your authority and therefore, your destiny.

DO NOT RECONNECT

When God frees you from a Laban, you do not reconnect--, not for closure, not for reconciliation, not for nostalgia. Freedom requires finality.

The blessing in Laban's house is proof of who you really are. The devil won't fight you unless you are about something and are onto something. Jacob's blessing grew in a hostile environment. That's how you know it was God, not circumstance. If your blessing only works in comfort, it's not God. If it multiplies in conflict, it's real.

The Lord prepares a table, in the presence of your enemies. (Psalm 23:5)

Laban's house was a pressure chamber, a training ground, a proving ground, and ultimately an identity revealer. As Jacob emerged as Israel.

"The Laban environment revealed strength, faith, capacity, and destiny you didn't know you had. And when the training was complete, God Himself pulled you out."

PROPHETIC DECLARATIONS

PROPHETIC ACTIVATIONS:

STEPPING INTO YOUR NEXT GOD-ORDAINED SEASON

This activation is meant to shift you from discernment to movement, from revelation to realignment, and from awareness to authority.

- Speak these aloud.
- Pray them.
- Declare them.
- Feel the atmosphere shift.

(To break old seasons and align with new instructions)

I declare by the authority of Jesus Christ:

- My spirit is awake.

- My ears are open.

- My discernment is sharp.

- My steps are ordered.

- My destiny is in motion.

I decree that:

- What God has closed, I will not reopen.
- What God has ended, I will not revive.
- What God has removed, I will not pursue.
- What God has released, I will not resist.
- What God has ordained, I will not delay.

I come out of every expired season.
I step into every appointed season.
I align with the timing of Heaven.

ACTIVATION: RELEASING THE OLD SEASON

Place your hand over your heart and speak this:

"Father, I release every place, person, assignment, mindset, and obligation You have freed me from.
I release old expectations.
I release old identities.
I release old fears.
I release old patterns.
I release old versions of myself."

Now take a deep breath and say: "What belonged to yesterday cannot follow me into tomorrow."

This is a spiritual exhale. A cleansing. A breaking of residue.

ACTIVATION: ALIGNING WITH GOD'S TIMING

Speak this next part slowly: "Lord, synchronize my spirit with Your timing. Let me be where You want me, with who You want me, doing what You want me to do, at the moment You desire it."

Now declare: "I will not be early. I will not be late.
I will not be stuck. I will not be rushed.
I will move at Heaven's pace."

ACTIVATION: CALLING IN NEW SEASON CLARITY

Repeat: "Father, reveal what's next. Show me where You are leading. Illuminate the assignment. Highlight the opportunity. Amplify the instruction. Magnify the path."

Then boldly declare: "I will see it. I will know it. I will recognize it. I will not miss my moment."

This is prophetic positioning — the ability to spot divine alignment when it appears.

ACTIVATION: BREAKING FEAR, HESITATION & DELAY

Lift your head, and say: "Fear will not hold me.
Hesitation will not bind me.
Delay will not sabotage me.

Doubt will not distract me.
I move with boldness, clarity, and courage."

Then declare: "I choose obedience over anxiety.
I choose faith over fear. I choose movement over stagnation."

This is the breaking of internal chains.

ACTIVATION: STEPPING INTO THE NEW SEASON

Now stand if you can — physically stepping symbolizes spiritually transitioning.

Speak this with authority: "I step out of old cycles.
I step out of spiritual confinement.
I step out of emotional captivity.
I step out of manipulative environments.
I step out of what no longer serves my destiny."

Then: "I step into purpose. I step into divine assignment. I step into breakthrough. I step into fresh oil. I step into my next season — fully."

Take one step forward. This seals the activation.

Say this loud and clear: "Heaven has shifted. The season has changed. My spirit agrees. My life aligns. My future opens. And I walk into what God has written — without fear, without delay, and without apology." Amen.

PROPHETIC ACTIVATION

Releasing manipulation & breaking its influence

This activation is for when you're ready to break every emotional hook, spiritual entanglement, and psychological pull that manipulators have established in your life — knowingly or unknowingly. Speak it aloud with authority. Atmospheres respond to sound.

DECLARATION OF IDENTITY -*This breaks the internal ground where manipulation grows.*

Place your hand over your chest and declare:

"I am not owned. I am not controlled. I am not obligated. I am not manipulated. I belong to God."

Say it again, slowly: "My voice is mine. My mind is mine. My decisions are mine. My destiny is God's."

You are reclaiming internal territory.

BREAKING INVISIBLE AGREEMENTS- Demons, devils and idol *gods* are sneaky. They can get you to agree to something and you don't even know that you did. You may not know that you agreed with anything or think that you agreed with something innocent that wasn't innocent at all. Therefore you must renounce all initiations and agreements, else these entities will think they have legal rights to operate in your life. Renouncing evil covenants and agreements is breaking them in the spirit. Amen.

Manipulation always forms silent agreements:
"Keep them happy." "Don't upset them." "You owe them." "Without them you are nothing."

Now declare: "I break every silent agreement formed under pressure, fear, guilt, or obligation."
"I break emotional contracts I never consented to."
"I break mental ties formed through manipulation, flattery, dependency, or fear."

Take a deep breath. You just dismantled spiritual machinery.

REJECTING FALSE OBLIGATION & GUILT

Say this firmly: "I reject false responsibility.
I reject manipulated loyalty. I reject weaponized guilt. I reject the lie that I must shrink to keep someone else comfortable."

Now speak this with authority: "I do not owe manipulators access, explanation, or continued presence."

This resets your boundaries.

CUTTING SOUL-TIES CREATED THROUGH MANIPULATION

Soul-ties aren't only romantic, they form through power, influence, dependency, fear, and emotional dominance.

Declare: "In the name of Jesus, I cut every soul-tie formed through manipulation."
"I cut ties with those who drained me, silenced me, or controlled me."
"I cut ties with the fear of their reactions."

Then: "Every emotional hook is broken.
Every mental leash is severed.
Every spiritual chain is shattered."

Take a symbolic motion of cutting with your hand.

PROPHETIC ALIGNMENT: CLEARING THE VOICE OF THE MANIPULATOR

Say: "I silence every voice that tried to shape my identity through control."
"I silence every voice that made me feel small, guilty, or obligated."
"I silence every voice that opposed my destiny."

Then speak: "Only God defines me. Only God leads me. Only God names me. Only God directs me."

Their voice loses power.
God's voice rises.

RESTORING YOUR SPIRITUAL REGISTER (DISCERNMENT)

Manipulation scrambles discernment. Now restore it:

"I command my discernment to sharpen.
I command my intuition to strengthen.
I command my spirit to hear God clearly."

Now declare: "I will not misread motives.
I will not doubt my discernment.
I will not second-guess divine direction.
I will not fall for familiar traps."

This is spiritual recalibration.

PROPHETIC RELEASE AND FORWARD MOVEMENT

Say: "I release every manipulator from my spirit.
I release every controlling influence from my mind.
I release every dominating presence from my emotions."

Now move your hands outward as if pushing away the old season: "I release fear. I release guilt. I release shame. I release confusion. I release emotional captivity."

Follow with: "I step into clarity. I step into strength.
I step into emotional sovereignty.
I step into spiritual authority." Take a step forward.

FINAL DECREES OF FREEDOM

Declare this loudly:

"I am free from manipulation.
I am free from fear.
I am free from control.
I am free from emotional bondage."

Then speak this prophetic decree that seals all of it:

"Every manipulative structure collapses.
Every controlling voice is silenced.
Every soul-tie breaks.
Every obligation dissolves.
Every chain falls."

And end with:

"I rise in clarity.
I rise in authority.
I rise in the fullness of who God called me to be."

Amen.

WARFARE PSALM - Against Narcissistic Manipulation & Controlling Spirits

O Lord, my Defender, hear my cry;
see the nets laid for my soul
and the snares woven by the proud.
Stretch out Your hand and lift me from the grip
of those who exalt themselves above others.

The narcissist speaks smooth words,
but their heart plots captivity.
Their praise is a cloak for control;
their kindness a mask for domination.
But You, O God, test every spirit
and expose every hidden motive.

They set traps for my peace
and call it love.
They twist truth for their advantage
and call it loyalty.
They burden my shoulders with guilt
and call it responsibility.
But You are the God who frees the oppressed
and breaks the yoke of false obligation.

Rise up, O Lord, and scatter every lying voice.
Silence the tongue that shames,

the mouth that belittles,
the whisper that confuses.
Cut off the influence of those who seek
to shrink my soul and dim my spirit.

My heart has been worn down by criticism,
my confidence bruised by manipulation.
But You, O God, restore my strength
and give me back my voice.
You lift my head where they cast it down,
and You call me Your own.

Break every chain they forged in secret;
tear every tie they wrapped around my mind.
Cut the cords of fear,
burn the ropes of intimidation,
and sweep away the residue of their control
with the fire of Your Spirit.

I stand upon Your truth, O Lord:
I am not owned by man,
nor controlled by their expectation.
I am Yours —
chosen, appointed, protected, and free.

Let the narcissistic spirit be as chaff before the wind;
let its schemes crumble like brittle clay.
Let the trap they set for me

become the pit they fall into.
For the Lord is my shield and my strong right hand,
my Guardian in the shadow of night
and my Light in the breaking of dawn.

Establish Your boundaries around me, O God;
hedge me in with Your peace.
Where they demanded access, close the door.
Where they claimed authority, revoke it.
Where they spoke curses, reverse them.
Where they sowed confusion,
command clarity to rise like the morning.

I walk forward unafraid, unhindered, undefeated.
The Lord Himself goes before me;
His Spirit strengthens my stride.
No manipulator shall reclaim me.
No controller shall rule me.
No narcissist shall bind me again.

For the Lord has spoken deliverance over my life.
He has shattered the yoke,
broken the leash,
and freed the captive.
His word is final,
His hand is mighty,
and His freedom is everlasting.

Bless the Lord, my Liberator,
my Advocate, my Fortress.
I will praise the One who restored my dignity

and returned my voice.
I will lift my hands to the God who saved me
from those who sought to dominate me.

Let this be my decree forever:
I am free, for the Lord has delivered me.
I am whole, for the Lord has healed me.
I am strong, for the Lord has upheld me.
And I walk forward in peace,
for the Lord Himself is my Keeper.

Amen.

DELIVERANCE PRAYER: BREAKING NARCISSISTIC CONTROL

Emotional, mental, spiritual, and relational freedom

This prayer is for when someone has dominated your emotions, controlled your identity, or manipulated your decisions. If they have made you feel small, guilty, or obligated, twisted truth, demanded loyalty but gave none, this prayer is for you. If they have punished independence, drained your confidence, shaped your self-perception through criticism or charm, then today, Today, that influence breaks.

OPENING DECLARATION

Father, in the Name of Jesus,
I come before You seeking total deliverance from every form of narcissistic control — emotional, mental, verbal, social, financial, and spiritual.

You are my Father, my Defender, my Counselor, and my Deliverer.

By Your authority, I renounce every chain that was formed through manipulation, charm, intimidation, guilt, false responsibility, fear, or emotional confusion.

Today, let me, help me, show me how to rise into freedom. **Amen.**

RENOUNCING THE SPIRITUAL ROOTS OF NARCISSISTIC CONTROL

In Jesus' Name, I renounce the following *spirits*:

the *spirit of domination*

the *spirit of intimidation*

the *spirit of confusion*

the *spirit of deception*

the *spirit of manipulation*

the *spirit of self-exaltation*

the spirit of control

the *spirit of emotional bondage*

the *spirit of fear*

and every *spirit* that hides behind false love or false loyalty

I reject every assignment sent to silence me, drain me, empty me, break me, weaken me, or to make me question my worth.

I renounce every spiritual tie created through narcissistic influence. In Jesus' Name. Amen.

BREAKING EMOTIONAL & PSYCHOLOGICAL BONDAGE

Now speak this firmly:

"I break every emotional hook. I break every psychological grip. I break every mental stronghold. I break every dependency bond. I break every fear-based connection."

I reject all internalized criticism, shame, unworthiness, guilt, lies about my value, and internalized responsibility for their reactions

I take back my voice. I take back my confidence. I take back my identity. I take back my emotional space.

CUTTING NARCISSISTIC SOUL-TIES

Soul-ties form through fear, intimidation, trauma, admiration, emotional domination. Obligation.

Declare: "In Jesus' name, I cut every soul-tie created through narcissistic control."
"I cut ties with words that wounded me, expectations that trapped me, and emotions that imprisoned me."

Then: "Every tie is severed. Every chain is cut. Every leash is broken. In the Name of Jesus."

DISMANTLING THE INTERNALIZED NARCISSISTIC VOICE

Narcissistic influence leaves a lingering internal critic. This is evident when their voice becomes your thoughts.

That ends now. **It must**.

Say: "I silence every internalized voice of criticism, belittling, dismissal, mockery, or shame."

"I silence the voice that told me: 'You're not enough.' 'You're too much.' 'You owe me.' 'You'll fail without me.' 'You're nothing without my approval.'"

Then declare: "I evict that voice from my mind and my emotions. Only the voice of God defines me."

RESTORING GOD-GIVEN IDENTITY

Say this next part slowly: "Father, restore my sense of worth. Restore my voice. Restore my dignity. Restore my confidence. Restore my strength. Restore my freedom. Lord, Restore my soul. In the Name of Jesus."

Then: "I am worthy of honor. I am worthy of respect. I am worthy of love. I am worthy of peace. I am worthy of safety. I am worthy of an abundant life. In the Name of Jesus."

You are undoing the identity damage.

DECLARATION OF DOMINION & BOUNDARIES

"I reclaim my emotional territory.
I reclaim my mental territory.
I reclaim my spiritual territory."

"I establish divine boundaries.
No narcissistic influence may cross them."

"Their power is broken. Their access is denied.
Their manipulation is exposed.

Their influence is canceled."

CLOSING WARFARE DECREE

Say this boldly:

"Every narcissistic stronghold collapses now.
Every controlling spirit is broken now.
Every counterfeit authority is stripped now."

"In the name of Jesus: I am free in my mind.
I am free in my heart. I am free in my spirit.
I am free in my identity. I am free in my destiny."

And finally: "I walk forward unhindered, unbound, unmanipulated, and undefeated.
The chains have fallen. The clarity has come.
The freedom is mine. In Jesus' name — **Amen**."

WARFARE PSALM For Breaking Soul-Ties

O Lord, my God, search my heart
and reveal every tie that binds me.
Show me the unseen cords
woven through emotion, memory, or longing.
Shine Your light upon every connection
that pulls my soul away from Your peace.

For some ties formed in love,
and others in loneliness;
some were born of kindness,
and others of manipulation.
But every tie that competes with Your voice,
Lord, break it with Your power.

There are those who left my life
but still live in my thoughts;
those whose hands are gone
but whose words remain.
They sit in my emotions uninvited,
their shadows rising when I try to stand.
But You, O Lord, reclaim the territory of my soul.

Cut every cord that drains my strength;
sever every tie that fogs my discernment.
Break every bond tied through fear,
through control,
through guilt,
through loneliness,
through trauma,
through desire,
or through misplaced loyalty.

Let every emotional chain fall.
Let every mental hook break.
Let every spiritual tether dissolve
by the fire of Your Spirit.
Let every imprint that does not come from You
be erased from my inner being.

For some ties were woven through words:
promises that never lived,
vows that were empty,
flattery that seduced,
criticism that wounded.
But Your word is higher than every false promise,
and Your truth is stronger than the lies that bound me.

Other ties came through touch,
companionship,
shared moments,
deep conversation,
and emotional intimacy.

But You are the Lover of my soul,
and You alone have the right to shape my heart.

Where I have given pieces of myself
without Your leading,
gather them back to me, O God.
Restore my fragments.
Reclaim my identity.
Rebuild what was scattered
by hands unworthy to hold me.

Where trauma tied me to those who hurt me,
break the cord of trauma-bonding now.
Where fear tied me to those who intimidated me,
burn the tie with Your holy fire.
Where hope tied me to those who deceived me,
untangle the snare with Your truth.

Let every false attachment
wither like a vine cut from the root.
Let every unhealthy longing
shrivel at Your command.
Let every soul-tie that competes with Your will
fall powerless at Your feet.

Teach my soul to breathe freely again.
Teach my heart to beat in rhythm with Your peace.
Teach my identity to rest in Your love
and not in the approval of another.

Surround me with Your presence, O Lord—
a hedge of fire, a mantle of purity, a shield of strength,
a wall of discernment. Let no old tie reconnect.
Let no severed bond reform.

I declare with the authority of heaven:
I am not tied to the past.
I am not bound to former seasons.
I am not entangled with those You have removed.
I am free from every soul-tie that is not of God.

My soul belongs to You alone, my heart to Your keeping, my future to Your writing. Heal the places that were tangled. Fill the spaces that were emptied. Restore the parts that were lost.

Bless the Lord, my Deliverer, my liberator and restorer. For He has severed the cords, broken the chains, and lifted me into peace.

This is my decree forever: I am whole. I am reclaimed. I am restored. And every soul-tie not sent by God is broken, burned, and buried —
never to rise again.

Amen.

HOW JACOB BROKE FROM LABAN

Jacob did five powerful things that every believer can replicate. First, he recognized the manipulation. Awareness is deliverance's first step. Jacob said, "He changed my wages ten times."

He received revelation from God who told him:

"Return to the land of your fathers."
(Gen 31:3)

Jacob didn't break free alone — God intervened.

Thirdly, he honored the boundaries God gave. He left secretly because that was the only safe option. Not all exits are loud; some are strategic.

Fourth, Jacob protected his household. He explained the truth to Rachel and Leah. They agreed he had been mistreated. Deliverance requires unified agreement.

Finally, he confronted the source directly. When Laban overtook him, Jacob finally spoke up:

> "What is my crime? What is my sin?"
> "You ransacked my camp!"
> "For twenty years I served you…"
> (Gen 31)

He confronted with truth, not fear. He established a new a line -- a boundary: The heap of stones, "Mizpah," signified that neither would cross this boundary again, each agreeing to say on their own side. He set a permanent spiritual boundary, and that is how generational cycles are broken.

DELIVERANCE PRAYER FROM LABAN *SPIRITS*

(Pray this with authority and clarity)

Father, in the Name of Jesus,
I renounce every Laban *spirit* assigned to my life — every *spirit of manipulation, control, deception, delay, and exploitation.*

I break the power of every spiritual contract, motional tie, or soul tie that was formed through oppression, confusion, or the misuse of authority.

I declare: I am not property. I am not owned. I am not controlled.

Every *spirit* of financial manipulation, emotional bondage, exploitation, narcissistic control, spiritual mixture, and household idolatry is broken off my life by the Blood of Jesus.

Lord, remove every residue of Laban's influence. Heal every place where my identity was suppressed. Restore my dignity, my voice, my clarity, and my confidence.

Just as You brought Jacob out with abundance,
bring me out with freedom, restoration, and increase.

I draw a spiritual boundary now — a Mizpah line —
between me and every manipulative influence.

What You have freed me from can never cross back
into my life. In Jesus' Name — Amen.

>Listen to GOD and speak to your work. speak to your labor. speak to your hands to be a wise steward and bless the orks of your hands. use the Wisdom of God to multiply your work.

SSTRENGTHEN YOUR STRENGTHS.

WARFARE PRAYERS

1. LORD, You are mighty. You are God. Lord, come to my rescue, see all that the *spirit* of Laban has done to me and help me out of this plight, in the Name of Jesus.

2. Evil *spirit* of Laban that has even taken all from his daughters and anyone else that has come into your house, including me, the Lord Jesus rebuke you. I bind this *spirit* that it has no further effect on me, in the Name of Jesus.

3. Evil *spirit* of Laban who has sold his children – his daughters to idols and who has devoured their inheritance and their money, the LORD Jesus rebuke you. I bind and paralyze this *spirit* that it has no further effect on me, in the Name of Jesus.

4. Any pursuing Laban ANY Laban riding or pursuing to accuse me…may a serpent bite your horse and overthrow you that you never catch me, in the Name of Jesus.

5. Whoever should accuse me of dealing falsely, of taking anything of theirs, people, children, animals, livestock, or their idol *gods*.

6. Anyone speaking a curse over me because of their idol *gods*, let the LORD silence you, unravel and dismantle that curse making it null and void against me, in the Name of Jesus. I do not want your idols; I am in Christ. Amen.

7. Anyone working knowingly or unknowingly to frame me or help a Laban frame me… the LORD Jesus rebuke you, in the Name of Jesus.

8. I have served Laban and served him well. *Spirit* of Laban whose house (business, office, farm, ranch, church or any other kind of enterprise) I have served in and you have denied, cheated and changed my wages multiple times, the Lord Jesus rebuke you and make you give me what is mine, in the Name of Jesus.

9. *Spirit* of Laban that wants to send me away when I must go or decide to leave and wants to send me away empty; the LORD Jesus rebuke you, in the Name of Jesus.

10. Any employer, former employer, boss, or spouse divorcing me who wants to send me and my children away empty, you are not of God; you are the *spirit* of Laban: the Lord Jesus Christ rebuke you, in the Name of Jesus.

11. Covenant maker- covenant breaker, contract changer, vow deny-er, the Lord Jesus rebuke you and make you pay what you promised, or double for

my trouble, or seven times more and let your stronghold be torn down, in the Name of Jesus.

Except the God of my father, the God of Abraham, and the fear of Isaac, had been with me, surely thou hadst **sent me away now empty. God hath seen mine affliction and the labour of my hands, and rebuked thee yesternight. (v 42)**

12. Anything that I am or have done that contributed to Laban having authority or control over me, I repent of it now, in the Name of Jesus. I repent to my mother, brother, father, sister... any relative, friend, or stranger, in the Name of Jesus.

13. Father, if You are using this manipulator to teach me, strengthen me, refine or grow me in anyway, I submit to Your process. Lord, forgive me for whatever I did to land in this predicament with a **manipulator**, in the Name of Jesus.

14. Lord, forgive, forget and remove all iniquity, all spiritual debt that allows this situation in my life, in the Name of Jesus.

15. Lord, forgive and remember the iniquity of my ancestors no more, in the Name of Jesus.

16. All other manipulators not of God, I reject you and bind you and ask the Lord to remove your source of power. I bind and paralyze those *spirits* and cast them out, in the Name of Jesus.

17. I reject all evil manipulations and manipulators, in the Name of Jesus, even if they appear to be in my favor, in the Name of Jesus.

18. Lord, let all evil manipulators against Your Will and against my destiny be rebuked, in the Name of Jesus.

19. I bind every evil *spirit* manipulating my benefactors, my destiny helpers against me ,in the Name of Jesus.

20. Destiny helper manipulations become powerless and ineffective, in the Name of Jesus. Lord, help my destiny helpers surround them with divine protection, a hedge of fire, a wall of fire, a mountain of fire, in the Name of Jesus. Make them--, make their lives and their purposes in my life too hot for the enemy, in Jesus' Name.

21. Father, in the Name of Jesus, make my blessings untouchable by any enemy, manipulator, or fake friend.

22. Lord, although my blessings may be delayed, I know what You have for me is for me and I will receive it in Your timing, in the Name of Jesus.

23. Every clever--, evil manipulator who looks like a friend, the Lord Jesus rebuke you, in the Name of Jesus.

24. Every clever, evil manipulator against me, the Lord bind your power and separate you from it, in the Name of Jesus.

25. Every guilt-tripping manipulator, I silence your words against me, in the Name of Jesus.

26. Every acting manipulator, I bind your outrage, your guilt, your fake victimhood – every mind game you play against me, in the Name of Jesus.

27. Lord, I set boundaries against the manipulators in my life and they must not pass lines I have set, in the Name of Jesus.

28. Lord, let me see through and ignore their anger, offense, and mind games, in the Name of Jesus.

29. Those who are not happy with my successes and independence, separate me from them, and them from me, in the Name of Jesus.

30. Fake friends, those who smile in my face, but seek my downfall, let them be frustrated and powerless against me, in the Name of Jesus.

31. Let everyone who seeks to control me, lose their power, lose their power, lose their power, in the Name of Jesus. Lord, render them powerless against me, in the Name of Jesus.

32. Lord, keep me from all evil wisdom, fake wisdom and alternative facts, in the Name of Jesus.

33. Lord, deal with any manipulator in my life from birth up to right now, in the Name of Jesus.

34. Anyone or anything, any *spirit*, devil, demon, or power that has dealt with me by manipulation from birth to childhood to teenage years to adulthood— using any part of my humanity, from placenta to hair, nails, blood – even dirt off my shoes, LORD rebuke them, remove them and reverse the effects of their evil against me, from birth up to now, in the Name of Jesus.

35. Lord, restore my soul. Lord, restore me. Lord restore my life of every damage, loss, evil reversal, caused by evil manipulators and manipulation, in the Name of Jesus.

36. Lord, break every evil bond, every evil soul tie that I may have with a manipulator, whether friend, foe, relative, false friend, or stranger, in the Name of Jesus.

37. Lord, remove any charm, amulet, or item that is manipulating my mind or life in any way, in the Name of Jesus.

38. Show me, tell me where it is, or what it is if I am to remove it myself, in the Name of Jesus.

39. If I am not to remove it, let it be utterly destroyed and burnt with Your fury and Holy Ghost Fire, in the Name of Jesus.

40. *Spirit* of Laban, fall down and die, in the Nname of Jesus.

41. *Spirit* of Laban, fall down and die out of my life, in the Name of Jesus.

42. *Spirit* of Laban, fall down and die out of my career, in the Name of Jesus.

43. *Spirit* of Laban, fall down and die out of my business, in the Name of Jesus.

44. *Spirit* of Laban, fall down and die out of my marriage and relationships, in the Name of Jesus.

45. *Spirit* of Laban, fall down and die out of my productivity and let go of the fruit of my labor, in the Name of Jesus.

46. *Spirit* of Laban, get out of my contracts and negotiations, in the Name of Jesus.

47. *Spirit* of Laban, you manipulator, fall down and die, in the Name of Jesus.

48. *Spirit* of Laban, get out of my family, in the Name of Jesus.

49. *Spirit* of Laban, get out of the people with faces that I am familiar with and who are familiar with me, in the Name of Jesus.

50. *Spirit* of Laban, stop sponsoring and empowering evil against me, in the Name of Jesus.

51. *Spirit* of Laban, be loosed from household people that I must deal with, in the Name of Jesus.

52. *Spirit* of Laban, I don't want your handmaidens—I rebuke and reject every strange woman or strange man sent into my life, in the Name of Jesus.

53. *Spirit* of Laban, I don't want your idols or your idolatry, in the Name of Jesus.

54. *Spirit* of Laban, get out of my camp, get out of my house, get out of my business, career, and office, I don't have your stuff, I don't want your stuff, and you are not welcome here, in the Name of Jesus.

55. *Spirit* of Laban, I don't want your children and I do not have your children, in the name of Jesus. Get out of my camp looking for your stuff—you can no longer have what is mine, in the Name of Jesus.

56. Any other evil *spirit* traveling with, attached to, or invited in because of the *spirit* of Laban, be bound, paralyzed and removed by Mighty Warrior Angels of God, now, in the Name of Jesus.

57. *Spirit* of Laban, I do not embrace your lust for money or your worship of mammon, in the Name of Jesus.

58. Anyone using me for their own advantage, the LORD Jesus rebuke them, in the Name of Jesus.

59. Anyone draining my efforts, my work, my plans, my success, the Lord separate me from them and

separate them from whatever source of power they are using, in the Name of Jesus.

60. Anyone planning to empty me for their own advantage, the LORD Jesus rebuke you, in the Name of Jesus.

61. All those who fake love me when I am useful, be exposed in the Light of God today, in the Name of Jesus.

62. All who are using our relationship only because it is useful and when it is not, I don't see them, I don't hear from them, separate from me today, in the Name of Jesus.

63. Unrepentant fake friends, evil friends, fake relatives who are always looking for their own advantage in what I do, what we do, whatever I'm working on – the LORD rebuke you, I reject you, now, in the Name of Jesus.

64. Users, you are all losers. I am the winner in my life because the Lord is on my side, in the Name of Jesus.

65. Tricksters, liars and truth deny-ers, the Lord Jesus rebuke you, in the Name of Jesus.

66. Lord, let all the affairs of my life remain a secret from manipulators and manipulation by evil, in the Name of Jesus.

67. My life, receive fire, become fire, in the Name of Jesus. (X3)

68. Lord, make my life too hot for the enemy to touch or handle, in the Name of Jesus.

69. Father, in the Name of Jesus, make my blessings untouchable by any enemy, manipulator, or fake friend.

70. Lord, although my blessings may be delayed, I know what You have for me is for me and I will receive it in Your timing, in the Name of Jesus.

71. Lord, expedite my deliverance and my blessings, in the Name of Jesus.

72. Father, let the glory of my destiny be their downfall, in the Name of Jesus.

73. Any power who looks on my life or destiny to do evil against it or me, let the brightness of my star that they are trying to steal make them stumble and fall, in the Name of Jesus.

74. Victims and fake victims, I reject you and your acting, in the Name of Jesus. Let your fake tears dry up. Put your pouting lips back to normal and don't pout against me, in the Name of Jesus.

75. I bind every demon of rage, or anger attempting to intimidate or manipulate me, in the Name of Jesus.

76. Those who try --, but can't use me, you will not guilt trip me, you are your own problem, not me and

I will not bend in any ungodly way or direction to please you or accommodate you, in the Name of Jesus.

77. Fake victims pretending to be hurt or wounded because you've been found out, make yourself scarce; hands off my life. The Lord Jesus rebuke you, in the Name of Jesus.

78. Wrongdoers hiding, pretending to be hurt or innocent when you are the evil one, the Lord Jesus put a stop to your fakery and your acting against me, in the Name of Jesus. Whatever evil spirit, entity or power that is empowering you, lose your power in the Name of Jesus.

79. Every manipulator, forget my name, lose my address, in the Name of Jesus.

80. Every manipulator manipulating my emotions, or attempting to do so, get away from me, and stay away, in the Name of Jesus.

81. Marriage manipulator: I am not your candidate in the Name of Jesus.

82. *Spirit* of Laban, I reject; I do not accept or want your marriage substitutes that you are sending in instead of the one God has intended for me, which is the one I want to marry and stay married to, in the Name of Jesus.

83. Marriage manipulator, you have **no** say so in who I marry, when I marry— my marriage covenant is with my spouse and GOD, therefore every evil manipulator, every evil, interloping, interfering *spirit*, power or other entity: get out of my marriage, in the Name of Jesus.

84. Marriage manipulators in the spirit realm and in the natural, lose your power; I send confusion into your camp, in the Name of Jesus.

85. Spiritual manipulators, I bind you, and the LORD Jesus rebuke every household wickedness, *spirit spouse* and every other anti-marriage force working against me and my marriage, in the Name of Jesus.

86. Every evil exchange against my marriage, be reversed, in the Name of Jesus.

87. Every evil substitution for my marriage, be reversed, in the Name of Jesus.

88. Lord, deliver my marriage from the hands of every evil interloper, in the Name of Jesus.

89. Lord, deliver my home from the hands of every evil interloper, in the Name of Jesus, whether I am related to them or not, in the Name of Jesus.

90. Lying manipulators, twisting my story for your own personal gain be silenced against me, my education, my life, my ministry, my marriage, my children and my destiny, in the Name of Jesus.

91. Evil directors in the natural or in the spiritual realm manipulating me and or others into jealousy, rivalry or comparison, lose your power against me, in the Name of Jesus.

92. Lord, I bind and reject the *spirt of jealousy*, it is a work of the flesh, and I reject it in the Name of Jesus.

93. Lord, I bind and reject the *spirit of rivalry*, competition and extreme competition; they are works of the flesh, in the Name of Jesus.

94. Lord, I bind and reject all covetousness, envy and comparison-*itis*, in the Name of Jesus.

95. I refuse unsanctioned hate or being pitted against another person, in the Name of Jesus. We do not war against flesh and blood, but against spiritual wickedness in high places.

96. Instead of competing with God's people, Lord, let God's people unite. Two can have a better reward, two or more can work together, pray together and bless the Lord and His people, in the Name of Jesus.

97. United we will stand, in Jesus' Name.

98. Father, do not let them divide what You have put together, in the Name of Jesus.

99. Lord, do not let the manipulator have rule over me and my life, in the Name of Jesus.

100. Lord, remove every spiritual debt in me and in my bloodline that gives place or license to any manipulator in my life, in the Name of Jesus.

101. Lord, have Mercy, forgive and remove all iniquity from my bloodline, in the Name of Jesus.

102. Lord, have Mercy and by the Blood of Jesus cleanse my bloodline and my foundation of every debt of manipulation and cleanse my foundation and bloodline of every manipulator in the spirit and in the natural, in the Name of Jesus.

103. Every triangulating power, every lying demon, I bind you and the LORD Jesus rebuke you, in the Name of Jesus. Those who tell multiple versions of stories – liars, you are not of God, the LORD Jesus rebuke you as it concerns me, in the Name of Jesus.

104. Lord, do not let any evil manipulator hide, either from You or me, in the Name of Jesus. Suspend their evil plans and works against me, and remove them from my life, in the Name of Jesus.

105. Expose the manipulators working against me, Lord. Don't let them hide from me, Lord – not in You.

106. Don't let them hide in the church, in the Name of Jesus.

107. Expose them, Lord, do not let them hide behind the words of the Bible which they may be able to

quote. If they are a manipulator or a liar, don't let them hide. Father, by the Holy Spirit and discernment, let me see them and Lord give me words to say and pray that they are removed from my life and their assignment against me is canceled, in the Name of Jesus.

108. Lord, when the strongman is caught, he must repay all he has stolen even up to sevenfold, in the Name of Jesus.

109. Father, do not let the strongman or any spirit, power, or entity go free even now that they have been caught, this manipulating *spirit* will deny wrong doing. They are a liar, make them repay in the Name of Jesus.

110. Lord, in the Courts of Heaven I accuse the accuser and ask for the Court's Mercy on me and the Court to deliver judgment and punishment against every evil manipulating *spirit*, devil, demon, power, or entity, in the Name of Jesus who is my Advocate and by the power in the Blood of Jesus which is my defense. Amen.

111. I nullify the effects of every evil manipulation in my finances, in the Name of Jesus.

112. Lord, let every evil manipulation against my spirit, soul or body—against my health and strength, comfort and clarity be stopped now, in the Name of Jesus.

113. Lord, let every evil hand working against my life receive Holy Ghost Fire, now, in the Name of Jesus.

114. Father, let every strange hand that has touched my life – any part of my life for evil, by manipulation, control, intimidation, or domination – let that hand wither by the power in the Blood of Jesus.

115. Father, any part of me or my life on any evil altar for evil manipulation--, by Your power, remove me from every evil altar, in the Name of Jesus.

116. Father, any part of me or my spirit soul or body in any lockdown, cell, jail, or captivity in any place in the entire universe, let Your mighty Angels search the land of the living and the dead and find me, locate me, and set me and my life free from every yoke, captivity, bondage, and manipulation, in the Name of Jesus.

117. I reverse every evil manipulation done against me, in the Name of Jesus.

118. Every deflector, detractor, distractor and deny-*er*, receive Holy Ghost slap and let the truth be in you now, or the Lord contend with you, in the Name of Jesus.

119. Shapeshifters, make-shifters, blame-shifters – LIARS, stop your lies and let go of me and my life,

in the Name of Jesus, by the power, in the Name of Jesus.

120. Every satanic monitoring camera or *spirit* monitoring me to manipulate my life or destiny, fall down and die, in the Name of Jesus.

121. Every serpentine manipulation of my life, fall down and die, wither, shrivel up and die, in the Name of Jesus. East Wind of God, blow them away from my life, in Jesus' Name.

122. Lord, let every selfish or satanic manipulation of my life that interferes with the timelines and the destiny You ascribed to me, let that manipulation fall to the ground as dead works, in the Name of Jesus.

123. Every evil manipulator watching me or crouched at the door of my life, home, or destiny to interfere with it, I cancel your assignment against me, in the Name of Jesus. The LORD Jesus rebuke you, in the Name of Jesus.

124. Every evil, lying, storywriter rewriting or attempting to rewrite the story of my life just to save your own hide or preserve your image, you are found out – LORD expose them and deal with them accordingly, in the Name of Jesus.

125. In the Name of Jesus, I come against the dark powers that have manipulated my relationships, friendships and courtships, and or marriage, in the Name of Jesus. Lord, destroy those powers so they do not rise up against me again, in the Name of Jesus.

126. Lord, remove every mind-controlling manipulation and all dream manipulations against me and my Godly relations, friends, and suitors, in the Name of Jesus.

127. Father, restore my name and reputation in the natural and in the spirit against all manipulators who have attempted to tear me down, in the Name of Jesus.

128. Father, restore my name, my reputation, my honor, in the Name of Jesus.

129. Lord, restore all my relationships, friendships, and courtships that should be restored, in the Name of Jesus.

130. Father, redeem the time, restore the years, in the Name of Jesus.

131. *Spirit* of Laban, you have no rights to my life, business ideas, or time, in the Name of Jesus.

132. *Spirit* of Laban, I do not owe you and you do not own me, in the Name of Jesus.

133. *Spirit* of Laban, my blessings are not yours, hands off, in the Name of Jesus.

134. *Spirit* of Laban, you do not own me, even if I accidentally or unknowingly went into your house. Even if you unknowingly helped me. I do not owe you and you do not own me. I renounce and denounce every and any agreement that I may have ever made with you whether I knew it or not, whether I realize it or not, whether you tricked me or not—you trickster. In the Name of Jesus.

135. Lord, forgive me for ever seeking or needing the help of Laban, forgive me, Lord for whatever I did that drove me to the house of Laban, in the Name of Jesus.

136. Lord, forgive me for lack of discernment. Forgive me for disobedience, rebellion, quenching or ignoring the Holy Spirit but instead going into the house of Laban or ever sitting at his table, in the Name of Jesus.

137. Lord, I denounce and renounce all sin and initiation related to Laban and the *spirit* of Laban, in the Name of Jesus.

138. Lord, forgive me if I tricked my brother out of anything, even his birthright and fled to the house of Laban. I remove my feet from Laban's house entirely. Lord, I remove my spirit soul and body from Laban's house; I have no agreements with Laban, in the Name of Jesus.

139. Laban's sister: I will not listen to you, I will not do what you suggest, you can not send me to the house of Laban; you are not my friend, helper, or close relative – even if you are, I will not go to the house of Laban, in the Name of Jesus.

127. Lord, let the house of Laban receive Holy Ghost Fire for the evil of that house, in the Name of Jesus.

128. For stealing from me, Send Your Angels to recover whatever is mine from Laban's house and send your divine scroll to destroy that house for evil

done against me, the lies and the thievery, in the Name of Jesus.

129. FAKE friend, Laban; you are not my friend, and I am not yours, in the Name of Jesus.

130. *Spirit* of Laban, you are not my family, and I am not yours, in the Name of Jesus.

131. I reject every demand from the *spirit* of Laban, in the Name of Jesus.

132. *Spirit* of Laban, I reject your fake public persona as you do evil to me, in the Name of Jesus. The LORD Jesus rebuke and judge you, in the Name of Jesus.

133. *Spirit* of Laban holding me back, I break loose. I break free from you by the power in the Holy Ghost and I escape your house forever, in the Name of Jesus.

134. Lord, Jesus separate me from the *spirit* of Laban and do not let my livelihood – not any part of it be attached to or tied to Laban, in the Name of Jesus.

135. *Spirit* of Laban: let go of my opportunities, in the Name of Jesus.

136. *Spirit* of Laban: if you are my boss or employer, let go of my pay, in the Name of Jesus.

137. Spirit of Laban you cannot change our agreement, contract or my pay again, in the Name of Jesus.

138. Spirit of Laban, let go of my money, in the Name of Jesus.

139. *Spirit* of Laban, I will not fall for your false promises again, in the name of Jesus.

140. *Spirit* of Laban, I can succeed without you; I am in Christ, you will not diminish my confidence in the LORD Jesus Christ, Amen.

141. *Spirit* of Laban, I reject your false *gods* and idols, I am in Christ, in the Name of Jesus.

142. *Spirit* of Laban trying to hold me back from breakthrough, the LORD Jesus Christ rebuke you; I will succeed, I will breakthrough, I will be free, and I will receive all the Lord has for me, even if He has to change my name, in the Name of Jesus.

143. Jealous Laban, jealous sons of Laban, sit down, the LORD Jesus rebuke you; sit down, in the Name of Jesus.

144. *Spirit* of Laban who can't celebrate my breakthrough, success, promotion, or increase, I see you, the LORD Jesus rebuke you, get out of my life, in the Name of Jesus.

145. Backbiting *spirit* of Laban, the LORD Jesus Christ rebuke you.

146. Lord, open great and effectual doors for me, in the Name of Jesus.

147. *Spirit* of Laban, shut your mouth with lies about all that you've done for me. I do not owe you. I am in Christ, and it is the LORD that is on my side who

has made me, kept me, provided for me, increased me, and blessed me, forever and ever Amen.

148. Lord, set a boundary forever between me and the *spirit* of Laban, in the Name of Jesus.

149. Lord, put a covenant between me and Laban that he must not cross the line of this Godly altar that has been established, and I call it Galeed and Mizpah.

> So Jacob took a stone and set it up as a pillar. He said to his relatives, "Gather some stones." So they took stones and piled them in a heap, and they ate there by the heap. Laban called it Jegar Sahadutha, and Jacob called it Galeed. [b]
>
> Laban said, "This heap is a witness between you and me today." That is why it was called Galeed. It was also called Mizpah, [c] because he said, "May the Lord keep watch between you and me when we are away from each other. …"
>
> Laban also said to Jacob, "Here is this heap, and here is this pillar I have set up between you and me. This heap is a witness, and this pillar is a witness, that I will not go past this heap to your side to harm you and that you will not go past this heap and pillar to my side to harm me. May the God of Abraham and the God of Nahor, the God of their father, judge between us." (Genesis 31: 45-53)

150. I seal these prayers, these words, these decrees and declarations across every dimension and timeline

with the Blood of Jesus and the Holy Spirit of Promise.

151. Every retaliation against these words, prayers, decrees, proclamations, declarations, against the speaker, the listener, and whoever prays these prayers at any time, from here into infinity, let it backfire without mercy on the perpetrator, from everlasting to everlasting, in the Name of Jesus.

Dear Reader

Thank you for acquiring and reading, this book. With this knowledge and prayers, you should receive deliverance from the spirit of Laban and every Laban in the natural, in your life.

Shalom,

Dr. Marlene Miles

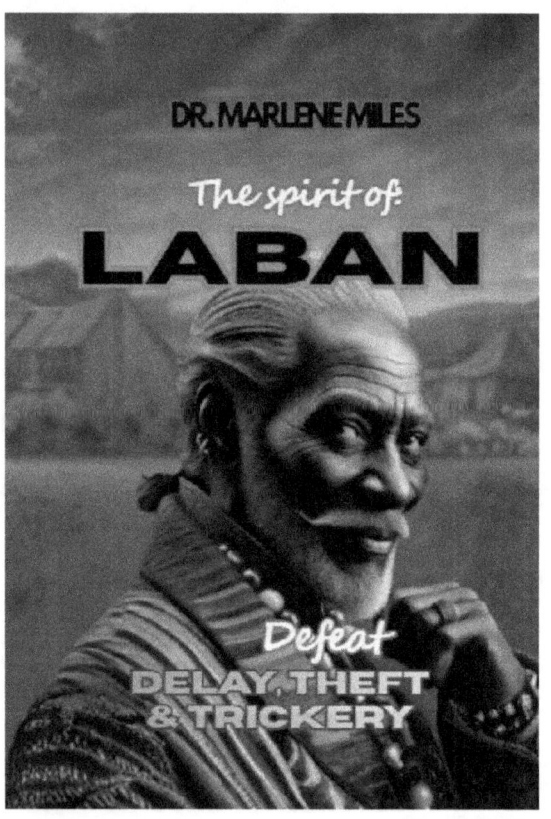

Prayerbooks by this author

While most books by this author have prayer points either throughout the book or at the end, there are some books that are only prayers. You just open up the book and pray.

Prayers Against Barrenness: *For Success in Business and Life*

Fruit of the Womb: *Prayers Against Barrenness*

Beauty Curses, *Warfare Prayers Against*
https://a.co/d/5Xlc2OM

Courts of Marriage: Prayers for Marriage in the Courts of Heaven *(prayerbook)* https://a.co/d/cNAdgAq

Courtroom Warfare @ Midnight *(prayerbook)*
https://a.co/d/5fc7Qdp

Demonic Cobwebs *(prayerbook)* https://a.co/d/fp9Oa2H

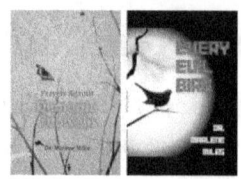

Every Evil Bird https://a.co/d/hF1kh1O

Gates of Thanksgiving

Praise Waits for Thee in Zion

So Thankful https://a.co/d/aePABdZ

Spirits of Death, Hell & the Grave, Pass Over Me and My House

Throne of Grace: Courtroom Prayer

Warfare Prayer Against Poverty https://a.co/d/bZ61lYu

Other books by this author

200 RED FLAGS: The Track Is Not Safe & workbook: RED FLAGS... How to spot red flags in relationships, especially in dating and romantic connections. https://a.co/d/ckyuqmb

Also. the **RED FLAGS** Workbook. Full size, ample room to write. Have a RED FLAG party with your friends and conquer relationship problems.

WE GET ALONG, RIGHT? *Compatibility Reality for Couples*. (book and companion workbook)

Companion Workbook: **WE GET ALONG, RIGHT?** *The Workbook for Couples Who Think They Do*

AK: The Adventures of the Agape Kid

Already Married in the Spirit: *Why You May Not Be Married in the Natural*

AMONG SOME THIEVES https://a.co/d/dkYT4ZV

Ancestral Powers

Anti-Marriage, *The Spirit of*

Backstabbers https://a.co/d/gi8iBxf

Barrenness, *Prayers Against* https://a.co/d/feUltIs

Battlefield of Marriage, *The*

Beware of the Dog: Prayers Against Dogs in the Dream.

Bless Your Food: *Let the Dining Table be Undefiled*

Blindsided: *Has the Old Man Bewitched You?* https://a.co/d/5O2fLLR

Break Free from Collective Captivity

Broken Spirits & Dry Bones

By Means of a Whorish Father

Caged Life: Get Out Alive!

https://a.co/d/bwPbksX

Casting Down Imaginations

Churchzilla, The Wanna-Be, Supposed-to-be Bride of Christ

Demonic Cobwebs (prayerbook)

Demonic Time Bombs

Demons Hate Questions

Devil Loves Trauma, *The*

Devil Weapons: Unforgiveness, Bitterness,...

The Devourers: Thieves of Darkness 2

Do Not Swear by the Moon

Don't Refuse Me, Lord (4 book series)
https://a.co/d/idP34LG

Dream Defilement

The Emptiers: *Thieves of Darkness, 1*
https://a.co/d/5I4n5mc

Evil Touch

Failed Assignment

Fantasy Spirit Spouse https://a.co/d/hW7oYbX

FAT Demons (The): *Breaking Demonic Curses*
https://a.co/d/4kP8wV1

The Fold (5-book series), The Fold (Book 1), Name Your Seed (Book 2), The Poor Attitudes of Money (3), Do Not Orphan Your Seed (4), For the Sake of the Gospel (5), My Sowing Journal

Gang Ups: Touch Not God's Anointed

Getting Rid of Evil Spiritual Food

https://a.co/d/i2L3WYQ

got HEALING? Verses for Life

got LOVE? Verses for Life

got HOPE? Verses for Life

got money? https://a.co/d/g2av41N

Has My Soul Been Sold? https://a.co/d/dyB8hhA

Here Come the Horns: *Skilled to Destroy* https://a.co/d/cZiNnkP

Hidden Sins: Hidden Iniquity

https://a.co/d/4Mth0wa

How to Dental Assist

How to Dental Assist2: Be Productive, Not Wasteful

How to STOP Being a Blind Witch or Warlock

I Take It Back

Legacy

Let Me Have A Dollar's Worth https://a.co/d/h8F8XgE

Let Them Come Up & Worship https://a.co/d/3yEAPMW

Level the Playing Field

Living for the NOW of God

Lose My Location https://a.co/d/crD6mV9

Love Breaks Your Heart

Made Perfect In Love

Mammon https://a.co/d/29yhMG7

Man Safari, *The*

Marriage Ed. Rules of Engagement & Marriage

Made Perfect in Love

Money Hunters: Beware of Those

Money on the Altar https://a.co/d/4EqJ2Nr

Mulberry Tree, *The* https://a.co/d/9nR9rRb

Motherboard (The) - *Soul Prosperity Series*

Name Your Seed

Occupy: *Until I Return* https://a.co/d/bZ7ztUy

Opponent, Adversary, or Enemy?: Fight The Right Battle with the Right Weapons

Plantation Souls

Players Gonna Play

Portals: Shut the Front Door: Prayers to Close Evil Portals.

Power Money: Nine Times the Tithe
https://a.co/d/gRt41gy

The Power to Get Wealth https://a.co/d/e4ub4Ov

Powers Above

The Robe, Part 1, The Lessons of Joseph

The Robe, Part II, The Lessons of Joseph

Seasons of Grief

Seasons of Waiting

Seasons of War

Second Marriage, Third--, *Any Marriage*
https://a.co/d/6m6GN4N

Seducing Spirits: Idolatry & Whoredoms
https://a.co/d/4Jq4WEs

Shut the Front Door: *Prayers to Close Portals*
https://a.co/d/cH4TWJj

Sift You Like Wheat

Six Men Short: What Has Happened to all the Men?

SLAVE

Sleep Afflictions & Really Bad Dreams
https://a.co/d/f8sDmgv

Soul Prosperity soul prosperity series 3

https://a.co/d/5p8YvCN

Souls Captivity soul prosperity series 2

The Spirit of Anti-Marriage

The Spirit of Poverty https://a.co/d/abV2o2e

Spiritual Thieves https://a.co/d/eqPPz33

StarStruck- Triangular Power series.

SUNBLOCK- Triangular Power series.

The Swallowers: *Thieves of Darkness*, 3

Take It Back

This Is NOT That: How to Keep Demons from Coming at You

Time Is of the Essence

Too Many Wives: *Why You Have Lady Problems*

Tormenting Spirits   https://a.co/d/dAogEJf

Toxic Souls

Triangular Power *(series)*, Powers Above, SUNBLOCK, Do Not Swear by the Moon, STARSTRUCK

Unbreak My Heart: *Don't Let Me Die*

Uncontested Doom

Unguarded Hours, *The*

Unseen Life, *The* (forthcoming)

Upgrade: How to Get Out of Survival Mode Toxic Souls (Book 2 of series) , Legacy (Book 3 of series)

The Wasters: *Thieves of Darkness,* Bk 2
https://a.co/d/bUvI9Jo

What Have You to Declare? What Do You Have With You from Where You've Been?

When I Was A Child, *I Prayed As a Child*

When the Devourer is Rebuked

https://a.co/d/1HVv8oq

WTH? Get Me Out of This Hell
https://a.co/d/a7WBGJh

The Wilderness Romance *(series)* This series is about conducting a Godly relationship and marriage with someone who is a Wilderness person. It is about how to recognize it and navigate through it. These books are about how not to get caught up in such.

- *The Social Wilderness*
- *The Sexual Wilderness*
- *The Spiritual Wilderness*

Other Series

The Fold (a series on Godly finances) https://a.co/d/4hz3unj

Soul Prosperity Series https://a.co/d/bz2M42q

Spirit Spouse books

https://a.co/d/9VehDSo

https://a.co/d/97sKOwm

Battlefield of Marriage, The

https://a.co/d/eUDzizO

Players Gonna Play

https://a.co/d/2hzGw3N

Sent Spirit Spouse (can someone send you a spirit spouse? This book is not yet released.)

Matters of the Heart, Made Perfect in Love
https://a.co/d/7OMQW3O , Love Breaks Your Heart
https://a.co/d/4KvuQLZ, Unbreak My Heart
https://a.co/d/84ceZ6M Broken Spirits & Dry Bones
https://a.co/d/e6iedNP

Thieves of Darkness series

The Emptiers https://a.co/d/heio0dO

The Wasters https://a.co/d/5TG1iNQ

The Swallowers https://a.co/d/1jWhM6G

The Devourers: Why We Can't Have Nice Things
https://a.co/d/87Tejbf

Spiritual Thieves

Triangular Powers https://a.co/d/aUCjAWC

Upgrade (series) *How to Get Out of Survival Mode*
https://a.co/d/aTERhXO

www.ingramcontent.com/pod-product-compliance
Lightning Source LLC
LaVergne TN
LVHW051558080426
835510LV00020B/3037